# Heal My Wounds, Leave My Scars

*A Mother's Story of Loss, Despair, and Her Journey Back to Hope*

Lorraine Reed Whoberr

Published by Hear My Heart Publishing LLC

Copyright 2018 by Lorraine Reed Whoberry

Written by Lorraine Reed Whoberry

ISBN: 978-1-945620-43-0
A product of the United States of America.

This book is a work of non-fiction.

*In loving memory of Stacie, in honor of Kristie, my beautiful daughters, our family, and all victims of crime!*

*"Nevertheless, there will be no more gloom*
*for those who were in distress.*
*The people walking in darkness have seen a great light;*
*on those living in the land of the shadow of death*
*a light has dawned.*
*You have enlarged the nation and increased their joy;*
*they rejoice before you as people rejoice at the harvest,*
*as warriors rejoice when dividing the plunder.*
*For as in the day of Midian's defeat,*
*you have shattered the yoke that burdens them,*
*the bar across their shoulders, the rod of their oppressor.*
*Every warrior's boot used in battle and every garment rolled*
*in blood will be destined for burning, will be fuel for the fire.*
*For to us a child is born, to us a son is given,*
*and the government will be on his shoulders.*
*And he will be called Wonderful Counselor, Mighty God,*
*Everlasting Father, Prince of Peace.*
*Of the greatness of his government*
*and peace there will be no end.*
*He will reign on David's throne and over his kingdom,*
*establishing and upholding it with justice and righteousness*
*from that time on and forever.*
*The zeal of the LORD Almighty will accomplish this."*

Isaiah 9: 1-8

# Contents

Chapter 1
# Total Darkness

The anticipation was excruciating. The ride was grueling. It was pitch black outside, and we were in the middle of nowhere--open fields in every direction. Would this event actually happen, or would it once again be postponed? No one had much to say. It was hard to focus. We could see the bright lights from miles away. After passing unmanned gates, the facility suddenly came into focus. We'd arrived. We were told to expect protestors and possibly supporters outside the main gate, but there were none. As we climbed out of the van, the two deputy sheriff's escorts said there were armed guards strategically placed, most unseen. An instant eeriness came over me, and the hair on the back of my neck stood up. I kept watching Kristie while holding tightly to my husband Richard. I silently prayed, asking the Lord to get us through the next hour.

We parked outside a small building with tin siding and roofing, which really didn't stand out in any significant way. It looked like all the other buildings on the grounds. The entire area was well lit like a football stadium. Razor wire circled the parameter.

While standing at the threshold of the open doorway, peering into the dark, cold, damp room, a strong stench assaulted my nostrils. I was told the smell would be horrendous. Words can't describe the odor. My body went rigid. My feet were paralyzed. I was overcome with an unrecognizable fear that surged through my body. My family was escorted into a room known as the *The Family Room*.

My daughter stood by my side unsure of herself and what to do. It was daunting, and I didn't know if I could take the next step. Kristie took my hand and said, "It's okay Mom; together we will get through this." She was right. I had promised her from day one, we would be together every step of the way. I would not back out now. This day was too important for us. We had waited eleven years for this day. Only, I wasn't the same person I had been on January 29, 1999. None of us were.

Kristie and I stepped into the room together, and it took a few seconds for our eyes to adjust before the steel door behind us slammed shut. We all jumped and froze right where we stood unable to see our hands in front of our faces. It was creepy and scary. Our eyes began to adapt. Gradually-the blinds opened, and an unfamiliar voice behind me spoke, "Mrs. Whoberry?" I responded with a faint yes, unable to take my eyes off the scene in front of me. I was numb and paralyzed to the spot where I stood. The gentleman introduced himself as the assistant warden of Greenville Correctional Institution. He said the event would take place at exactly nine p.m., which we were already aware of. By the department's standards, we had been well informed. By our standards, we were not prepared, nor would we ever be.

We stood behind a one-way mirror looking into the stark white room: The death chamber. L Unit was seated deep inside the sprawling compound of Greenville Correctional Center in Jarratt, Virginia. The death chamber was brightly lit. I recognized staff from the Attorney General's and Governor's office. One gentleman stood by the red phone located on the wall outside our room and directly to our right inside the death chamber. I kept a close eye on the phone, anticipating it would not ring. I had it on good authority Virginia Governor Tim Kaine, who was against the death penalty, would not interfere. Kristie needed to know there would not be any more postponements.

Keeping my eye on the clock and listening to the chaos inside the death chamber, I kept reassuring myself "this too shall pass" while holding tightly to my daughter Kristie and my husband Richard, shaking uncontrollably, and anticipating the outcome.

The media room was to the left of our room, facing the death chamber. The media witnesses were already seated when the curtains opened.

At 8:53 p.m., we heard a muffled voice. The assistant warden noted that the chaplain was reading Mr. Powell his last rights. A few short minutes later, we heard the rattling of chains. The assistant warden didn't bother to explain. The rattling chains grew louder, indicating he was coming down the hall

At 8:55 p.m., he stepped into view, handcuffed and shackled. He was escorted by four large prison guards. With his head held high and wearing typical correction garb, a faded blue button-down collared shirt, blue baggy pants with the left leg cut off at the knee, rubber flip flops, no belt, and his head shaved, he shuffled toward the solitary wooden chair. Standing and facing the witness room, he waited while the prison guards unshackled him. His eyes turned in our direction. We were standing behind the one-way mirror. He sat down in the chair and was strapped in with leather straps. The peace in his eyes gave me reassurance. A guard wet his bare left leg and strapped a metal band around it.

Before the leather mask was placed over his face, he was asked if he had any last words. He said nothing and never diverted his eyes from our direction. His face was covered with a mask with only his nose showing. A metal cap was strapped on his head.

A guard standing inside the death chamber in the far right rear of the room, turned a key activating the system. A high-ranking corrections staff member known only to the warden, concealed in an adjoining room, hit the "execute" button. It was precisely nine p.m.

There was a thump as Powell's body jerked back in the chair. His hands clenched into tight fists and curled as his body strained against the force of the electricity. His veins swelled as his body turned blood red. Smoke rose from his exposed leg. He was jolted with 1800 volts at 7.5 amps -- about 13,500 watts that flowed through his body for thirty seconds, followed by 240 volts at one amp for sixty seconds. The cycle repeated. With the second major jolt, smoke and sparks emitted from Powell's right leg. His knee swelled and turned purple. His knuckles went white, and his body went limp.

At 9:03 p.m. the electricity stopped. Everyone waited in complete silence while his body cooled down enough for the doctor to check for a pulse. It seemed like an eternity. At 9:08, a guard walked up to Paul and opened his shirt. A doctor placed a stethoscope on Paul's chest in search of a heartbeat. There was none. He was pronounced dead at 9:09 p.m., and the curtain was drawn.

Chapter 2
# A Parent's Worst Nightmare

*"A horrible and shocking thing has happened in the land."*
Jeremiah 5:30 (NIV)

Our day began as any other typical Friday morning; I woke the girls for school and got ready for work. Kristie was always the hardest to arouse. She liked to linger in bed for as long as possible, especially on cold, wintery days, and that particular Friday was one of those.

Kristie turned fourteen in December and preferred riding the school bus. Being an eighth grader, it wasn't cool to be seen being dropped off at school by your mom. I hugged and kissed Kristie goodbye that morning and told her I loved her and headed out the door. Stacie, sixteen, liked to catch a ride with me, as she didn't like riding the school bus. I cherished this time we had together each morning.

I kissed Stacie goodbye and told her I loved her as I dropped her off at school. How could I have known as I watched her walk away that it would be the last time I would see her alive: The morning of January 29, 1999. In a few brief hours, our lives would change forever.

Later that afternoon, Stacie called me around noon to let me know she was home; she had early dismissal due to final exams and was going into work early for extra hours. Stacie was working her first job at Popeye's Chicken, and she was excited! She was very outgoing and loved people, and being the new kid on the block, she wanted to prove herself while making some extra money.

She promised she would get her chores done, and if she didn't finish, she would have them done by Saturday morning.

I called the house an hour later to talk to her but got no answer. Assuming she had left for work, I paged her, but she didn't return my call. Not wanting to bother her on the job, as lunch time gets quite busy, I decided to call her later, as we didn't have cell phones at that time.

When she had received her first paycheck, we'd opened a savings account and bought a pager. She'd been working about four weeks and was doing very well with the responsibilities of balancing school and work.

That afternoon was the last time I spoke to Stacie believing everything was okay. I waited for Kristie to call and let me know when she arrived home from school, which normally came around 3:15 p.m. Kristie's call never came. . . . *It's three thirty, why hasn't Kristie called me? She should be home from school by now. Where is she?* I thought again. I paged Stacie, but she never returned my call.

Thinking Kristie's bus was late, I finally called the school, but it was after 4:00 p.m., and everyone had left for the weekend. Bobby, my fiancé, usually arrived home a little after four. I waited for his call to let me know all was well, as was the routine. His call never came. At 4:55 p.m. my personal line at my desk rang, but it was an unfamiliar voice.

## Chapter 3

# "9-1-1. What's Your Emergency?"

*"God is our refuge and strength, an ever present help in trouble."*
Psalm 1:46 (ESV)

### Actual 9-1-1 call from Bobby ~ January 29, 1999
### (Approximately 1620 hours)
### Manassas, VA

Operator: "This is the county 911. What is your emergency?"
Bobby: "Hello, 911?"
Operator: "Hello, hello?" The phone went dead.
(Bobby has to find another phone, as this one was off the charger too long. Bobby redials 911.)
Operator: "This is the county 911. What is your emergency? You need to talk to me; you can't make a call."
Bobby: "Hello."
Operator: "You cannot make a call without talking to me first."
(Bobby didn't realize the call went through, he was still dialing.)
Bobby: "Hello ma'am?"
Operator: "Yes."
Bobby: "I got a 911. I got two kids down."
Operator: "Okay."
Bobby: "Don't, don't -- get through this."

Operator: "Sir you need to calm down, I have no idea what you are talking about."

Bobby: "Okay, who is this?"

Operator: "911. What do you need?"

Bobby: "Okay, your 911?"

Operator: "I can barely understand you; your phone is all scratchy. What's the problem?"

Bobby: "Okay, I got two kids; one's been, looks like she's been shot, and the other been, throat's been cut."

Operator: "Do you have a different phone? I cannot understand you."

Bobby: "Okay just a second."

Operator: "Your phone is full of static."

Bobby: "Just a second ma'am. You're okay Kristie; stay there Kristie. Just a second ma'am, okay, no I don't. Can you hear me?"

Operator: "I can hear you a little better now. Who is in your, what's going on?"

Bobby: "Okay I, one girl, my girl, one girl's been, looks like, she's been shot and. . . ."

Operator: "Who?"

Bobby: "My daughter."

Operator: "Your daughter what? What do you mean with a gun?"

Bobby: "Yes ma'am. I just got home, and the other one's upstairs. I didn't get to check her very good."

Operator: "Where is your daughter?"

Bobby: "Okay, she's in my basement, in my house."

Operator: "Okay."

Bobby: "You ready, who do I call? Please."

Operator: "Okay, does she, I guess she needs an ambulance then too?"

Bobby: "Yes ma'am."

Operator: "But you don't know what happened?"

Bobby: "No ma'am. I just came in; I don't know nothing that happened either. She's barely talking, and the one upstairs is not talking."

Operator: "So she's not conscious?"

Bobby: "Yes the little one is."

Operator: "Okay."

Bobby: "Ma'am hurry up, please."

Operator: "Okay, just stay on the phone with me a minute okay? I need to get some more information from you."

Bobby: "Okay, ma'am."

Operator: "Okay."

Bobby: "It's okay, Stacie."

Operator: "Now."

Bobby: "Okay, Kristie, ma'am hurry please."

Operator: "Okay, how old is the daughter that looks like she's been shot?"

Bobby: "She is fourteen."

Operator: "Okay and what is, are you getting any information from these kids?"

Bobby: "No she can barely talk. Her throat's been cut, ma'am."

Operator: "Her throat has been cut?"

Bobby: "Yes ma'am."

Operator: "Okay, why did you say it looks like she, she's been shot?"

Bobby: "She got a bullet hole, it's either, or stab wound or bullet hole in her stomach -- ma'am she, she's barely hanging on."

Operator: "Okay sir."

Bobby: "You're okay, Kristie."

Operator: "Stay with me, okay?"

Bobby: "You're okay, Kristie; you're okay; can you talk hun?"

Kristie: (Moaning.)

Bobby: "No."

Operator: "Okay, where's the other daughter?"

Bobby: "She's upstairs on the top floor in her room. I didn't see any cuts or any signs on her, but she is unconscious."

Operator: "Okay, could okay she, the daughter upstairs in unconscious?"

Bobby: "Yes ma'am. Please ma'am."

Operator: "Okay I under, I understand your upset sir."

Bobby: "Help me."

Operator: "I just need you to stay on the phone with me okay? I've already sent it forward to be dispatched."

Bobby: "Okay."

Operator: "Okay?"

Bobby: "Now the youngest one."

Operator: "Okay, and how old is your other daughter?"

Bobby: "She's sixteen."

Operator: "And your sixteen-your-old is unconscious?"

Bobby: "Yes ma'am. I'm, I'm down with the youngest one right now. The oldest one, she's unconscious. I don't know if she's breathing or not. I just came downstairs, and that's when I met my other."

Operator: "Okay, are you the only one home?"

Bobby: "Check the whole house."

Operator: "Are you the only one with the two children?"

Operator: "Okay, is this Robert?'

Bobby: "Yes ma'am."

Kristie: (Moaning.)

Bobby: "Okay. You're okay honey."

Operator: "Okay, we are gonna get units out there to you."

Bobby: "Okay, but pretty soon somebody is coming out?"

Operator: "Yeah, and there's, you're the only one with both children?"

Bobby: "Ma'am as far as I know."

Operator: "So you can't get to the sixteen year old?"

Bobby: "Ma'am, I don't want to leave this my."

Operator: "I understand that; that's why I'm asking you; you are, you the only one home right now?"

Bobby: "As I know of, yes."

Operator: "As far as family."

Bobby: "Yes ma'am, yes ma'am."

Operator: "Okay and the sixteen year old is upstairs unconscious?"

Bobby: "Yes ma'am. You're okay Kristie, don't talk, you're okay."

Kristie: (Moaning.)

Operator: "Okay, and the fourteen year old, her throat has been cut?"

Bobby: "Yes ma'am."

Operator: "And it appears that she has been stabbed?"

Bobby: "Yes ma'am-- please yes, don't be scared honey. It'll be okay. You're going to be okay Kristie; don't be scared."

Operator: "And you're the father sir?"

Bobby: "I'm the fiancé, I'm sorry."

Operator: "You're the Robert, you're the fiancé? Where, where's the Mother?"

Bobby: "Their mom's at work; I haven't been able to call her."

Operator: "And she appears to have been stabbed?"

Bobby: "Yes ma'am, in the stomach right above the belly button."

Operator: "Okay, is she conscious?"

Bobby: "Right."

Operator: "Not very?"

Bobby: "Not very, ma'am."

Operator: "Okay."

Bobby: "Hold on Kristie; you're okay; okay, just hold on; don't talk; you're okay; you're okay."

Operator: "Okay, does it look like someone broke into the house sir?"

Bobby: "Ma'am I couldn't tell. The door was open when I came in."

Operator: "Okay, so you're really, you're not sure what exactly is going on. You came home from work and found them that way?"

Bobby: "Yes ma'am, it's scaring me; her feet are tied together; she's got shoe laces all around."

Operator: "Okay, wait a minute, whose feet are tied together?"

Bobby: "My thirteen, my fourteen-year-old."

Operator: "Your fourteen-year-old?"

Bobby: "Yes."

Operator: "Feet are tied together?"

Bobby: "Yes ma'am; it doesn't look good."

Operator: "Okay, and so you have no clue the status of your sixteen-year-old, because she's upstairs."

Bobby: "Yes."

Operator: "Is that correct?"

Bobby: "Yes, ma'am."

Operator: "Okay, you don't know if someone's still in the house?"

Bobby: "Ma'am I don't know, I don't know. Oh my God, you're okay, Kristie, okay. Just hang on."

Operator: "Are you there, you're there with the fourteen-

year -old?"
Bobby: "Yes, ma'am. Did you see who it was?"
Kristie: (Moaning.)
Operator: "Okay, can you reach any clean cloth that is close to you? Is there anything that you can grab, a clean towel?"
Bobby: "I got, I've got a pair of sweats that. . . or a tee shirt."
Operator: "Okay, anything clean, I want you to grab that for me."
Bobby: "Okay, hold on, Kristie, hold on, don't try to talk."
Operator: "Okay, and you said she's got a cut on her throat right?"
Bobby: "Yes ma'am, real bad."
Operator: "Okay, I want."
Bobby: "Multiple cuts."
Operator: "Okay listen to me. I want you to put the clean cloth, whatever it is that you have. I want you to put it over her throat, and hold it there and apply pressure to it, okay?"
Bobby: "Okay, over her throat?"
Operator: "Yes."
Bobby: "Kristie, you're gonna be okay, okay Kristie."
Operator: "And if it becomes blood soaked. . . ."
Bobby: "Does it hurt?"
Kristie: (Moaning.)
Bobby: "Just lay down."
Operator: "Okay, Robert listen to me."
Bobby: "Yeah."
Operator: "If it becomes blood soaked, I don't want you to remove it."
Bobby: "Okay."
Operator: "I want you to keep it on her."
Bobby: "You're okay Kristie."
Operator: "Okay, and if it becomes blood soaked. . . ."

Bobby: "What's that?"

Operator: "I just want you to find something else to put over that one okay?"

Bobby: "Be here in a few minutes okay. I'm sorry ma'am what was that?"

Operator: "Okay, if the cloth on her neck becomes blood soaked, I want you to go ahead and take another one, put it right over top of that."

Bobby: "Okay."

Operator: "Do not remove what you put there."

Bobby: "Got you."

Operator: "Okay and you don't know where the Mom is?"

Bobby: "No, she's at work. I haven't been able to call."

Operator: "Okay, so the Mom's at work?"

Bobby: "Yes, ma'am."

Operator: "Okay."

Operator: "Okay, what's the Mom's name?"

Bobby: "Lorraine."

Operator: "Lorraine?"

Bobby: "Yes ma'am. Dispatch, if you want, tell them to use the back door to the porch."

Operator: "To use the back door?"

Bobby: "Through the porch, they can use any door, but the back door was already open."

Operator: "Okay, and the back, hold on one second, stay on the line with me."

Bobby: "Okay, you're okay Kristie; just stay there, okay, just stay there, when this, when did this happen honey?"

Kristie: (Moaning.)

Bobby: "Okay, don't talk, okay?"

Operator: "Can you hear the sixteen-year-old at all? Can you, is she calling out to you?"

Bobby: "Ma'am, I can't hear, no."

Operator: "You can't hear anything?"

Bobby: "No ma'am."

Operator: "Okay."

Bobby: "Please, please, please!"

Operator: "Okay, is she, is she conscious still, your fourteen-year-old?"

Bobby: "Yes, yes she is, my fourteen-year-old is still conscious."

Operator: "Okay, just try not to let her talk to you okay?"

Bobby: "Kristie, you don't talk, okay?"

Operator: "And you said it appears she has been stabbed in the chest or the stomach or?"

Bobby: "In the stomach above her belly button."

Operator: "In the stomach above her belly button?"

Bobby: "Yes ma'am."

Operator: "Okay, can you tell me, does it appear she is bleeding profusely from her stomach?"

Bobby: "No. She's just got a little bit of a trickle. Keep your hand down Hun."

Operator: "Okay, she's just bleeding a little bit from her stomach?"

Bobby: "Can I put, uh, something over her, her body a little bit?"

Operator: "Yeah, go ahead."

Bobby: "She's starting to shake a little."

Operator: "If you can grab a blanket without letting go of her, yes, you can go ahead and cover her to keep her warm. She's probably going into shock."

Bobby: "You're okay, Kristie; don't move; you're okay, okay. I done this ma'am; are you there?"

Operator: "Yes, I'm here. I'm not going to hang up till we get officers there. We -- looks like we got an officer out front, but I'm going to stay on the phone until they're actually inside your house."

Bobby: "Thank you because I heard someone."

Operator: "It's probably the officer because we have an officer marked out there. They're just probably out front."

Bobby: "Okay, that's just my cat; I got two cats in here. It's okay Kristie; they're here okay; they're going to be down in just a little bit okay? They'll be down in just a little bit. Tell her."

Unknown: (Loud yelling.)

Operator: "Is an officer there?"

Bobby: "Yes. Downstairs. They are here, okay. That's them, that's them!"

Unknown: (Loud yelling.)

Bobby: "Yes. Downstairs."

Operator: "Tell her they are in the basement?"

Officer: "Where are you?"

Bobby: "I'm downstairs. As you come down the steps, I am to the right."

Operator: "Is the sixteen-year-old on the main level of the house?"

Bobby: "Yes ma'am."

Operator: "She's on the main level of the house where they came in. Yes, that's what he knew when he left her. He's with the fourteen-year-old."

Unknown: "He's downstairs."

Bobby: "I'm downstairs."

Officer: "Right here, right here, right here. Tell the fire board to come on now, now, now."

Operator: "Okay are you with an officer?"

Bobby: "Yes, I have an officer here ma'am."

Operator: "Okay, I'm going to go ahead and disconnect the phone, okay?"

Bobby: "She can barely talk; her throat's been slit."

Operator: "Okay, I'm going to go ahead and. . . ."

Officer: "Tell her to lay still; I have somebody coming."

Bobby: "I have one upstairs in the bedroom. As you're going down the hallway, it's the first room on the right. I'm sorry, the left."

Officer: "First over on the. . . ."

Operator: "Okay sir?"

Bobby: "Yes."

Operator: "Okay, now, is where the other daughter, are the fire units there yet?"

Bobby: "I haven't moved yet; I don't know. Um, she asked for, to send somebody in, so I guess they are. Are you going to call their mom, or am I?"

Operator: "Okay, okay you just let the officer know; let the officers know where Mom is, okay?"

Bobby: "Okay."

Operator: "Okay, we, I'm going to go ahead and hang up with you okay? We will get fire units to you there shortly."

Bobby: "Alright, thank you."

Operator: "Okay? All right, bye-bye. Oh my God, what a weird call."

Chapter 4
# Sweet 16

*"A woman giving birth to a child has pain because her time has come; but when her baby is born she forgets the anguish because of her joy that a child is born into the world."*
John 16:21 (ESV)

After twenty-three long hours of labor, Stacie Lynn entered the world at 4:24 p.m., weighing 7lbs and 6oz. Stacie was the fifth of five living generations born of her maternal family consisting of Great-Great-Grandma Maxwell, Great-Grandma (aka Nana), Grandma (aka Meme), Mom (me), and Stacie. It was something I was proud of, having also been a fifth generation member of my paternal and maternal family lineage.

August 21 signified a special day in our family history. Stacie shared this day with two of her great-great maternal grandmothers: Grandma Johnnie Maxwell, born 1898, and Grandma Orishus Cooper, born 1882, one hundred years earlier.

She was a beautiful little girl with the finest, blondish hair and big blue eyes -- God's precious gift!

On August 21, 1998, one hundred years later from her Great-Great-Grandma Maxwell's birth, we celebrated Stacie's sixteenth birthday. Stacie was an Elvis fan and grew up on the music of the fifties and sixties, which set the tone for her birthday party, a 1950's theme. Meme made the girls poodle skirts. Nana came and spent the week with us, which made it even more special. We held Stacie's party in a neighborhood park, so the girls could invite all their friends.

Stacie was the life of the party. She danced to "oldies but goodies" songs and made the party fun. It was a very special day because it was the last birthday we would ever celebrate with her! My only regret was not realizing how special it truly was. Not only would her birthday become a treasured memory, but the forthcoming holidays that year would be as well. For that Thanksgiving, Nana and my sister, Theresa, and her family came and spent a week with us! Since living in Virginia, this was the first visit for my sister and her family.

With one holiday behind us, Christmas was approaching, and the girls were getting really excited. One memory stands out vividly. A co-worker and dear friend invited us to join them to cut down a live Christmas tree. The girls were giddy with excitement as we drove to the Blue Ridge Mountains of Virginia.

With a convoy of five vehicles, we drove to a tree farm, picked up our saw, and headed out in search of the perfect tree. It was unusually warm that day. After walking a while, we decided we'd found the one. Kristie decided she would cut it down. After a few strokes with the saw, she'd had enough. Stacie tried and lasted only a few minutes. The other families were working on their trees, so it was up to the three of us to cut ours down.

It took us almost two hours, but Stacie finally conquered it. Both girls realized simultaneously that we were going to have to drag it all the way back to the truck! At this point, cutting down a tree wasn't so fun after all; it was a lot of hard work.

But they persevered, and we drug it all the way back, only to discover it was as big as our little truck. The guys at the farm secured it, and off we went. When we arrived home, I told the girls to leave it on the truck until Bobby got home. That evening Bobby took it and put it in a bucket of water. He commented on what a big tree it was.

We all four stood there staring at it and Stacie said, "It's perfect."

Kristie commented, "It didn't look that big when we cut it down; did it grow?" We laughed and told the girls it needed to sit there for several hours and soak.

Bobby and I were on a bowling league, and normally, the girls would go with us and hang out with friends. We should have known when they asked to stay home that they had already devised a plan. A few hours later, we returned home, but neither of us noticed the Christmas tree was missing until we entered the house and found it standing in the corner. The sight was hysterically comical. Out of the bottom of the tree, stuck Kristie's legs, frantically waving. We heard Stacie giving directions, "Move it to your right," but she was nowhere to be seen. Kristie yelled back at her sister, but neither one realized we'd walked in and that we're watching.

It's clear they needed some help, but we decided to let them work it out between themselves. We silently laughed ourselves silly while watching the girls struggle. It was so tall it wouldn't stand up straight and so big around it took up a good portion of the corner of the room, blocking the television.

Stacie was pinned in the corner behind the tree, and Kristie was underneath. We rescued them taking the tree back outside, which took both of us to move it. It was amazing they managed to get it in the house by themselves. We trimmed and cut and trimmed some more until we got the right fit.

Who knew a real tree could be so much fun? The girls couldn't wait to start decorating. They were so proud of themselves and that tree!

My mom and step-dad spent Christmas with us that year. It was another great holiday with lots of memories.

Chapter 5
# Hopes and Dreams

*"Sing to the Lord a new song for he has done marvelous things!"*
Psalm 98:1a (ESV)

On the wall of Stacie's bedroom hung her calendar, marking off the days until the big event. The Osbourn Park High School Military Ball was the topic of the week and scheduled for February 6. The countdown was on with nine days to go. Stacie talked non-stop about the upcoming event. Her excitement was contagious. Stacie lived life as an adventure, and she made her high school days fun. February 6, 1999, couldn't get here fast enough for her. It would become a special day but not as we had planned. However, it would be a day we would *never* forget. . . .

Stacie reminded me daily of the hair and nail appointments that *had* to be scheduled. "Mom, we have to find the perfect shoes; when can you take me?"

Jokingly, I said, "Stacie, I know the perfect pair of shoes--combat boots." She smiled a very mischievous smile, which could only mean one thing—she was seriously considering it.

"My gown is black; they would match," she said. However, she didn't own combat boots, thank goodness. But with only nine more days left, we had to find her a pair of shoes.

Stacie and her friends decided to go Dutch on a limousine for the night! Memories were waiting to be made and dreams were yet to come true.

Stacie was not a girly girl. She was somewhat of a tomboy, yet she embraced life and lived every moment to the fullest! At sixteen and a freshman in high school, she had discovered a whole new world unexplored. Not long after school started, she shared with me that after she graduated, she wanted to join the Navy! Since joining the NJROTC program, she had found her calling in life. I was totally shocked.

Wow, my daughter was talking about joining the Armed Services to serve her country. She continued, "I'm going to become the first female Navy Seal!"

As surprised as I was, a pride swelled inside of me, and I hugged her, encouraged her, as any parent would do, and prayed for her! "God, protect this precious young woman and the Navy because she's going to turn the world upside down." Like most teenagers, she didn't like rules and was still testing her boundaries.

These were big dreams! We encouraged her to follow those dreams. As a parent, it's sometimes hard to step aside and give kids the freedom they so desperately seek as they learn who they are and who the Lord is creating them to be.

In February of 1998, almost a year prior, my finance' and I had moved into our dream home in Yorkshire, a suburb of Manassas, Virginia, a quiet, serene neighborhood and perfect for our family. Our house was the neighborhood hangout. It was good knowing where the girls were and who they were with. Stacie was always bringing new friends home. I took each opportunity to get to know them. Or at least I thought I had.

McLean Street is a long narrow two-block lane. The neighborhood, established in 1962, consisted of half-acre lots and ranch-style homes. This house was everything we wanted: A basement for our workshops, a family room, three bedrooms, and dining and living area.

We especially enjoyed the screened-in sun porch, where we sat and watched the different species of birds, the squirrels, the beautiful flower beds, and our garden. Less than a year later, our lives would be forever changed.

## Chapter 6
# Kristie's Rescue

*"Out of the depths I cry to you, O' Lord."*
Psalm 130:1 (ESV)

Bobby arrived home from work a few minutes after four and found the back door unlocked and no mail. The girls always kept the doors locked when home alone and picked up the mail after school. He walked into the kitchen to call me at work to let me know he was home, but the phone was missing. Assuming Stacie had left it in her bedroom, he made a mental note to check there after checking the mailbox. He recalled she was scheduled to work at three. He wasn't aware she had planned to go in earlier.

He retrieved the mail, came back in, and walked down the hall past Kristie's room to Stacie's room; he was shocked to find it in disarray. Her full-length mirror was lying on the hardwood floor shattered. Her bed was sideways and pulled away from the wall, the sheets were gone, and the mattress askew. There were items strewn across the floor, and things were out of place. It wasn't like Stacie to leave her room messy. He thought to himself, *It looks like a fight has taken place in there.*

He looked around for the phone but didn't find it. He turned and left her room, and as he passed back by Kristie's room, he discovered Stacie lying inside the doorway in a pool of blood. He ran and knelt beside her, calling her name, while frantically trying to revive her.

Her eyes were open, but she was unresponsive. "Oh God! Oh God!" he cried out.

He knew he had to get help immediately. He hadn't found the phone as of yet. He jumped up and ran down to the basement stairs, "Explicit! Explicit!" He stopped! He thought he had heard his name called. No, he must have imagined it. Stacie was unresponsive. He took a few more steps.... He had heard his name called; there was no doubt that time! It sounded muffled and strange, and he thought it came from the basement. He ran into the basement and found our three bicycles lying in a heap with Kristie beneath them, nude, and bleeding with her hands tied behind her back and her feet bound. He threw the bikes off of her and knelt down beside her, uncertain as to what to do. There was blood everywhere, and she was extremely pale.

"Oh my God!" he shouted.

She had a look of terror written all over her face. It was suddenly obvious; the girls had been attacked. He realized she couldn't speak; her throat had been slashed, and she had been stabbed in the stomach. She desperately was trying to talk to him. She kept moving her eyes and trying to move her body, but he didn't understand and told her to lie still. He was afraid to touch her for fear he might hurt her, but he knew he needed to stop the bleeding, and he needed to call 9-1-1, but the phone was still missing.

He knelt beside her, finding a shirt lying nearby from a pile of laundry and applied pressure to her wounds. Her hands and feet still were bound with shoelaces.

Another thought paralyzed him; the attacker could still be in the house. He reached over and grabbed a log from the woodpile and placed it beside him.

Kristie struggled to talk, trying desperately to convey her terror. He told her he was going to get help! She tried to convey to him not to leave her alone. She kept tilting her head back and rolling her eyes as if she were trying to tell him something. He turned and looked in that direction, and lying on the dryer was the cordless phone. He grabbed the phone and dialed 9-1-1. He remembered Stacie lying upstairs and was uncertain she was dead or alive.

The emergency operator answered, "9-1-1. What's your emergency?" The phone beeped and their call was disconnected. The phone went dead.

Kristie was in severe shock and was rapidly fading.

He said to her, "I'll be right back. I need to get another phone."

She pleaded to him with her eyes and moaning, which could be heard on the 9-1-1, not to leave her alone as she watched him disappear from her sight! She listened as time seemed to stand still. She tried to call out, but she had no voice. She was terrified the monster would kill Bobby and return to finish her off.

Chapter 7
# Time Stood Still

*"You meant evil against me, but God meant it for good."*
Genesis 50:20 (ESV)

Traffic in Northern Virginia on a normal day is horrendous. Friday evenings were worse. A fifteen-mile-drive home sometimes took an hour and a half, but if there was an accident, it could take two to two and a half hours to get home.

I was straightening my desk to leave for the weekend, when my personal line rang. *Finally*, I sighed. My family decided to check in with me. I answered, only to be greeted by an unfamiliar voice.

"Ms. Reed?"

"Yes," I replied, somewhat taken aback. The caller introduced himself as a Prince William County police officer. "How can I help you, officer?" The thought that something could be wrong never entered my mind.

"Ms. Reed, when are you coming home?" He asked.

Surprised at the question, I didn't respond right away. He caught me completely off guard with his inquiry, and I wasn't prepared to answer such a strange and straight forward question. So I inquired, "Why?"

He hesitated for a brief period and said calmly, "We need you to come home."

"Okay. I'm heading out the door in a few minutes." He

did not seem to be worried, alarmed, or nervous. He gave me no indication anything was wrong. I politely said again, "I will be on my way shortly." After another long, quiet pause, I asked if he was still there. He answered with another question, asking how long it would take me to get home. I advised him that since it was 5:00 p.m. on a Friday, during rush hour, and I was coming from Chantilly to Manassas, it could take anywhere from an hour and a half to two hours, depending on traffic. He causally said "Okay," again with no alarm in his voice.

I still was unsatisfied with no explanation as to why he needed me to come home. So once more I asked what this was all about. There was another long period of silence for what seemed like an eternity. I thought he had hung up, and then he said coolly, "We just need you to come home."

Okay, I'd had it, and this conversation was ridiculous; I was getting upset. I said, "Yes sir, we've established that, but I need you to explain what this is all about!"

Again, he hesitated. Finally, he said, "Well, we have your daughter!"

"Okay." *Great! What am I going to have to deal with when I get home?* I thought. T*he kids were probably playing basketball, and one of them broke a neighbor's window while playing basketball in the driveway.* I asked him which daughter he had with him because I have two. His reply shocked me.

"We don't have a name."

Without hesitation I replied rather sharply and loudly, "Then how do you know she's my daughter?" There was another long silence. By now I'd had it with the officer, but I needed answers. Sighing and recomposing myself, I gave him a brief description. "Is she tall and slender, long blonde hair and wears braces?"

"Yes," he said unconvincingly.

"Okay, I've just described both my daughters to you? Which one do you have?"

Silence.

Completely fed up, I finally said to him, "This conversation is going nowhere. However, you called me, and yet, I'm asking all the questions? What is wrong with this conversation?"

He apologized profusely and, in a pleading voice, asked me to please come home.

In an abrupt response, I said, "I'm on my way, and I will be there as soon as I can." I slammed the phone down and quickly gathered my belongings to rush out the door, thinking *What an idiot!*

On the way out the door, I said my goodbyes to girls in the office. One co-worker noticed I was slightly agitated and asked if I was okay to which I astutely replied, "The police are at the house waiting on me, and I have to get home."

She replied, "Oh boy, good luck." We all lightly laughed it off. As parents themselves, most of them had been there at least once with their kids.

I drove home with the radio on as usual, but my mind was stuck on that conversation, or lack of, with the officer. I wasn't concentrating on the radio.

Thank God for the protection over me. If I had been listening, I would have heard the horrific news broadcasting the attack of two sisters, raped and murdered in Yorkshire. I was later told by friends who heard the same broadcast that both of the girls' names were given by the press. It was big news, and it was their job to report it, without regard to the family or the victims. They had no concern for the fact that perhaps the family hadn't been notified or might be listening and that most of the information they were giving was incorrect.

The Lord distracted my attention away from the radio. If I had heard it, I would have left a scene of destruction fifteen miles long, seriously injuring, if not killing, those in my path, as well as myself.

That conversation with the officer kept playing over and over in my mind. *Why didn't he know my daughter's name? Why was he so vague? Was he intentionally avoiding my questions? If so, why? None of it made any sense.*

Suddenly, it all started coming together; the unanswered phone calls. No contact with any of my three family members in the past five hours. I became nauseated and very upset. Something was terribly wrong!

Traffic was bumper-to-bumper and backed-up for the fifteen miles I needed to travel to my turn off, and it wasn't moving anytime soon.

Everyone must have known I desperately needed to get home quickly and decided to drive in slow motion. Route 28 is a four-lane road divided by a median with lights at every intersection. It's grueling, causes tempers to fly, people cut you off, and patience runs thin. Yet, it was just another typical Friday evening in Northern Virginia. The drive under normal circumstances takes well over an hour.

I would learn later from putting together the time frame, I made it home that day in twenty-nine minutes, which is a record in and of itself. It was by the grace of God and only by the grace of God I made it home in such a short amount of time, unscathed and without harming anyone else. God parted the Red Sea on Route 28 that fateful day.

Chapter 8
# The Face of Evil

*"Why should I fear when evil days come, when wicked deceivers surround me—?"*
Psalm 49:4 (ESV)

The girls and I never had the opportunity to shop for those perfect pairs of shoes. And the hair and nail appointments were never fulfilled. All Stacie's hopes and dreams reflected the shattered mirror that lay on the floor in her bedroom. In the blink of an eye, everything changed. What I wouldn't give to go back to that day listening to Stacie talk about her future -- to hold her and hear her voice once more. Our lives lay shattered in pieces -- jagged, broken in a million pieces.

Evil-morally, reprehensible, sinful, and wicked was the ugliest and darkest place the human mind can fathom. The agony of hell is real. I see it. I feel it, and yet it's a horror I never could have imagined. . . .

On January 28, 1999, evil boldly walked into our home in an attempt to destroy all our lives. The evil that terrorized our family appeared as a normal-looking human being. Our family lived in hell in our own home. By appearance, he looked like your average person only he was disguised as a young man with a troubled past and a history of misdemeanor crimes, however, nothing as big as the crime he was about to commit. Paul Warner Powell, a twenty-year-old transient became our worst nightmare.

On January 28, Kristie called me at work around three thirty that afternoon, inquiring when I would be home. That was a strange question as she knew our work schedules. I told her I would be home between six and seven.

I detected something in her voice; she sounded different, almost scared. I asked her what was wrong. She said, "Nothing." But I knew my daughter. She needed something. I asked her again what was wrong. She was whispering that one of Stacie's friends was in the house, and *he* wouldn't leave! I immediately became suspicious and started asking questions. Kristie doesn't reveal information; you have to pull it out of her.

"Who is this person?" I asked.

"Paul." She said softly.

"Paul. Who is Paul?" I asked. I made a point to know all the girls' friends and thought I did, yet this name didn't sound familiar. "Where does he live?" She didn't know. "How old is this person?" She thought he was nineteen. "Where is Stacie?"

She replied, "At work."

"Who *is* this person, and what is *he* doing in our house?" I was both angry and scared. This person was in my house alone with my daughter. I asked Kristie where he was.

She said, "He's down the hall going through all the rooms."

I said to her, "Get out of the house and stand on the front porch and talk to me; don't hang up!" I told her to stay on the front porch and tell that person I said, *"Get out of our house, NOW!"* She relayed the message in her frail, scared voice.

I waited a few seconds and asked her what he was doing. She said he was leaving out the back door. I told her once he was out of the house, go in, lock the doors, and wait for us to get home. She did!

If anyone came to the door, she was not to open it and call the police. I knew Bobby would be home shortly. I'd planned to talk to Stacie when she got home from work that night about this Paul person. Unfortunately, she had burned her fingers at work and called me a few minutes after closing, crying hysterically. I rushed to pick her up. Her fingers were blistered. I took her to the pharmacy to pick up supplies to doctor her hands. It was late when we arrived home, and once I got her settled down, I completely forgot about the incident. There was a storm coming, and I would suffer an enormous battle of guilt.

Chapter 9
# The Death Notification

*"Even though I walk through the valley of the shadow of death, I will fear no evil, for you are with me; your rod and your staff, they comfort me."*
Psalm 23:4 (ESV)

As I approached the next to the last turn before turning onto McLean Street, I was very distraught over the phone call I had received. I struggled to calm myself down and push all those horrible thoughts from my mind. I wanted to believe it was something minor. My heart was pounding, my palms begin to sweat, my stomach was queasy, and my head was throbbing. I was a nervous wreck. I tried to convince myself everything would be fine.

And yet, as I turned onto our street, I couldn't believe the scene before me. I was stunned! As I sat staring down the long lane, dusk had settled, and one dim street light gave a shadow of light. Our street was utter chaos. I was sitting at a road block, and all traffic was prohibited. There was nowhere to go. I waited anxiously, watching as a police officer ambled toward me. He didn't seem to be overly excited to see me. I assumed he would know who I was once I told him my name and address. After all, it was one of his fellow officers who had called and asked me to come home.

While watching the chaos, I felt I had stumbled onto a movie set. But the faces of people milling around brought me back to reality. Something was terribly wrong. I noticed numerous fire trucks, ambulances, police cars, and telephone company trucks all parked askew as far as I could see down the long lane. I noticed a large bus parked in our neighbor's driveway with officers milling around it. It turned out to be a police command unit.

The officer causally inquired how he could help me. I gave him my name and said I received a call from an officer who asked me to come home. He asked my address, which I gave him again.

He told me to wait there, turned, and walked away, talking into his radio. I couldn't hear the conversation. He was in no hurry and took his time. I didn't understand why he wasn't giving me some direction, and why was it taking so long? I needed to get home and check on my girls. I was looking upward for smoke, thinking a neighbor's house might be on fire, and we could be in jeopardy. But there was no smoke. I looked over to my right and found Kristie's friend, Markie, standing alone, looking confused and distraught. His parents lived across the street and next door to where the command unit was parked. I got his attention and asked him what was going on. With tears in his eyes, he said, "They're not telling me anything."

Before I could respond to him, the officer returned and said, "Pull over and park." He seemed agitated with me. What had I done to upset him? I thought since the police had called me to come home, this officer would know what I needed to know and offer to help me.

Years later our paths would cross again. When I asked him about that night and why he had brushed me off, he said there were several reasons. He hadn't anticipated having to deal with me, and then he needed to find out what to do with me, while trying to compose himself before he could come back and talk to me. All he could think of was to instruct me to pull over and park. He had three daughters and this case had shaken him to the core.

I pulled up a few feet, parked on the right side of the street, jumped out of the truck, and began running down the street, zig zagging between parked cars.

I stopped short, "Oh No! There is yellow police tape around my house! *MY HOUSE!*" I said out loud to no one.

Out of nowhere came a blur of blue. I was surrounded by uniformed police officers. Two officers took my arms and led me away in the direction I had just come from. "No!" I screamed. "I need to find my girls." I kept trying to pull away. "Let me go! I need to find my girls!" I couldn't fathom why I was held and led away from my house and family.

I was taken into a neighbor's home, a family we didn't know. Police officers were packed inside the house. I was pushed forward with nowhere to go. I was released and hit by dozens of questions all at once.

"Where are my girls?" I demanded. I needed to find my girls! No one heard me.

Everyone talked at once, and I couldn't decipher their words or make sense of the madness. I didn't understand. What had I done? Everything happened so quickly; it became a blur.

The officers continued asking question after question. I closed my eyes, hoping they would vanish and shouted at the top of my lungs, "STOP! Be quiet! I can't understand everybody at once." It was finally quiet. I felt someone touching me again.

I opened my eyes to find a small photo right in front of my face of some man I didn't recognize held by an arm coming from over my shoulder, asking, "Ms. Reed, do you know this man?"

The photo was so close I had to lean back to focus. "NO!"

"Your daughter identified him." My head was spinning. "What do you mean my daughter identified him? Which daughter? Where are my girls?"

The crowd shifted, and I spotted Bobby sitting on the sofa with his head in his hands. *Was he there the entire time?* I pushed my way over to him. "Bobby, where are the girls?" He was unresponsive. His eyes were red and glassy. *What was wrong with him?* "Bobby?" I said again, loudly over the crowd. Everyone stopped talking, and all eyes were on us. No one said a word.

I grabbed Bobby, and I began pleading with him to tell me where the girls were. He looked right through me. He didn't respond. I shook him and asked him again. He looked at me and, in a voice I didn't recognize, said, "Stacie's gone."

In mother mode, I started in. "Gone? She knows better than to leave without asking permission. Where is she? Who's she with? When did she leave? When is she coming home? Why are all these police here?"

A police chaplain suddenly appeared and placed his hand on my shoulder and calmly said, "Ms. Reed, you need to sit down."

I screamed back at him, "I don't want to sit down, tell me where Stacie and Kristie are."

He said very softly, "Everything is going to be okay."

I snapped back at him, "What is going to be okay?"

I hadn't noticed that most of the officers had left the house, leaving Bobby, a police officer, the police chaplain, and me alone. The silence was deafening. I kneeled down in front of Bobby, and he came back from wherever it was he had been. He looked at me with tears streaming down his face, crying uncontrollably. I held his hands and waited for him to tell me what was wrong. Finally, after what seemed like hours, he looked at me and said, "Lorraine, Stacie's been murdered."

I couldn't answer him. I couldn't move. I couldn't breathe. If I wasn't already sitting down, I would have collapsed. I was thrown into an instant state of shock. My body refused to move, and my mind wouldn't accept the news. He put his arms around me and sobbed hysterically. I couldn't cry. I was numb. My body was paralyzed.

I jumped up. "Oh no! Where's Kristie? I need to find Kristie. She is supposed to be home, but she never called me after school. Where is Kristie?" I looked around at the officer and the chaplain, "Where's Kristie? We need to find Kristie. I need to go find her!"

In my mind, I was walking to the front door. However, I hadn't moved; my body was still paralyzed. I was still standing in front of Bobby, searching for answers.

The chaplain came over to me; I will never forget the look in his eyes. He said, "Kristie was flown to Inova Fairfax Hospital and is in surgery."

I remember staring up at him in complete and utter disbelief. "No, Kristie is at home, and I need to go to her. She needs me now! I remember feeling as if I were standing outside my own body. I had difficulty reacting to what the chaplain was saying. I couldn't cry, I couldn't scream, I couldn't move. I was told later I was in complete shock.

After what seemed like an eternity, in reality was only a few seconds; my mind instantly began the denial process. "This isn't happening. This is a horrible nightmare. My girls never hurt anyone. Why would someone hurt them?"

The chaplain looked at me with tears in his eyes and said, "Ms. Reed, everything is going to be okay. Let me know if there is anything you need."

*Anything I need?* I'm shouting in my mind, but the words won't come. I can't utter a single word.

Grief affects everyone in different ways. The human mind is sometimes impossible to understand. The chaplain was doing his best to comfort us in his mind. The only officer in the house still with us had mentally checked out a long time ago. Bobby was folding. I was silently screaming at all of them.

"How is everything going to be okay? Someone has murdered Stacie, my child, who was only sixteen-years-old. My mind flashed back to her sixteenth birthday party. She hadn't learned to drive yet. She was only beginning to date. She was beautiful and so full of life. She had just started her first job. She was in her first year of high school. The thoughts were like a movie playing out in my mind. *NO! NO!* I silently screamed, but no one could hear.

When I was finally able to speak, I looked at Bobby and pleaded with him to take me to Kristie. "I need to get to Kristie. I need to make sure she is okay. We need to go wherever she was taken." He looked at me like I was crazy.

Through tears, he whispered, "She was flown to Inova Fairfax Hospital" He hesitated. "She's not expected to live." I had no idea the toll it took on him. I had no idea that it was he who had found Stacie dead upstairs on Kristie's bedroom floor and Kristie lying on the cold cement floor in the basement, bound, nude, bleeding to death, and in shock.

"NOOOOOOOOOOOOOOO! NOOOOOOOOOO!" I wasn't hearing this. "You're lying; you're wrong. I can't lose both my girls! NOOOOOO!" At some point, I had knelt down on the floor again, and I remember picking myself up with great effort to leave. I would drive myself to the hospital. I was looking for my keys.

The officer intervened and said "Ms. Reed, we are working on getting you both to the hospital as soon as possible. Neither of you are in any condition to drive."

Unbeknownst to us, we were being intentionally delayed. The police were trying to rule out the possibility that we were involved. We had no idea we were potential suspects. This was so surreal. *How could this happen to us? We didn't' deserve this. My girls didn't deserve it. Why Us?*

At that moment, I couldn't awaken from that horrible nightmare, and I desperately wanted to wake up. The only problem was, I was awake, and it was real and was happening.

The chaplain came over to me again and put his hand on my shoulder. He told me *again*, "Everything is going to be okay."

I blew up at him. "You keep saying that. How is everything going to be okay? Stacie has been murdered, and Kristie is fighting for her life and not expected to live. I may never see or talk to her again. Tell me how everything is going to be okay?"

With his head down, he turned and walked away. The officer quickly stated he was going to check on the car. The chaplain decided to follow the officer and give us time alone.

A few moments later, the officer returned and asked Bobby to step outside with him. They left, and I was all alone, feeling like a caged animal and pacing the floor, trying to come up with a plan of escape. My mind was in turmoil; my body was in agony and not coping well with the situation at hand. Waiting was excruciatingly painful.

The lady of the house appeared and introduced herself as Colleen Fisher. She expressed her condolences and graciously asked if there was anything she could do or that I needed.

Though I don't recall the entire conversation we had, I do recall her asking if she could pray with me! "Yes! Please!" (I get goose bumps every time I think about her precious words). God sent His angel, Colleen, and she prayed for us. That was a comfort I will never forget.

She asked about my family. "FAMILY! Oh no, my family." It hadn't occurred to me to call them. They were all in Texas. She asked me for their phone numbers, but I couldn't remember anyone's number. My mind wouldn't function. She was very patient with me, and I gave her my mom and sister's names. She called information and got their contact information.

I called my mom in Weatherford, and her answering machine picked up. I couldn't just leave a message, so I called my sister, Theresa, in Fort Worth. As soon as she answered, I said in a shaky and unfamiliar voice, "Theresa, put Chris on the other phone." She asked who was calling. She hadn't recognized my voice.

I said, "It's me, Lorraine." She immediately asked what was wrong. I begged her to please put Chris on the other line, so I could tell them together. Chris picked up, and I began to fumble through what little details I knew. Theresa cried! I asked her if she knew where Mom was. She didn't know. I asked her to please get everyone to Nana's house.

I couldn't bear the thought of Nana being told over the phone while she was alone. She was seventy-four-years-old. She had lost her youngest son, Ricky, in 1969 at the age of sixteen. He was killed along with his sixteen-year-old girlfriend, Nita, by a drunk driver. She had buried two husbands and too many family members. She needed to know about Stacie and Kristie, her great-granddaughters, but family needed to be there with her when they delivered the news.

I called my mom a second time, and she picked up. It was heart-wrenching to deliver such horrific news over the phone and to be so far away. I gave her the tragic information and that we were desperately trying to get to the hospital. I also asked her to please call the family together to meet at Nana's house to deliver the news to her in person. Mom was very distraught, but I gave her the name of the hospital, told her I loved her, and I promised to call her later. After hanging up, I felt incredibly alone. I was very thankful to Colleen who graciously opened her heart and her home to us. I am forever grateful for her faith, strength, compassion, and friendship.

Time seemed to stand still. The officer who had taken Bobby from the house came back after a while and said they had a car ready to take us to the hospital. I jumped up and ran to the door, down the steps to the waiting car outside. The chaplain was seated in the front passenger seat of the police cruiser. Bobby was in the back seat. I climbed in behind the chaplain, anxious to leave.

And yet, we didn't leave right away. Instead we sat and waited and waited and waited. The officer and the chaplain carried on a conversation as if they were long lost buddies and hadn't seen each other in a long while. "How's the wife? How are the kids? The weather hasn't been too cold lately." That conversation between the two is engraved in my mind as if it were yesterday. I remember how it grated on my nerves like sandpaper in an open sore.

The car was running, and I asked several times, "When are we leaving?"

"Shortly," came the same short and curt reply. I felt I was intruding on their conversation. Finally, I looked at Bobby and asked him to get us there.

Just as I reached for the door handle to open my door of the police cruiser, the officer was called on his radio, and he left the cruiser. We sat and waited again for an eternity. It was so dark out, I couldn't see anyone. The darkness swallowed everyone around us. After a few minutes, the chaplain said he would go find the officer. I think he was tired of me asking when we were leaving.

Bobby and I sat alone in the car. It was quiet, yet our hearts raced in anxious anxiety. We were startled when Bobby's door opened; an officer asked Bobby to follow him. Once again I was all alone, sitting there desperately looking for someone to help me. *What was going on? Why was I left alone? Why were we still parked here instead of leaving for the hospital?* I felt like a caged animal. Nobody seemed to care about our pain, torment, and anguish, or that we needed to get to Kristie before it was too late. *Where was Kristie? Was she still alive? Was she all alone? Would I make it in time to see her before she passed away?*

I glanced around the cruiser and spotted the keys in the ignition, and it was running. My mind began to race. *There was no partition between the back/front seats. What was keeping me from jumping into the front seat and driving myself to the hospital?* I thought, *I have to move quickly.* Just as I had placed my hands on the front seat to climb over, my door opened, and there stood yet another police officer. I had not seen this particular officer before. He asked me to step out of the car.

I remember thinking that car must have been defective, so I was being taken to another vehicle. Instead we walked down the street, weaving in between other vehicles toward my house. It's strange that although I knew we were heading toward my house, I didn't question the fact that they didn't take me in, nor do I remember walking past the house. I was shown to another vehicle and climbed into the passenger seat of an unmarked police car.

A plain-clothed officer introduced himself as Detective Richard Leonard, the master detective handling the case. He stated he needed to ask me a few questions. I somberly agreed. He asked about the girls' friends. He needed their names, phone numbers, addresses, and parents' names. I advised, "I can't recall any of the information at this moment, but there's an address book in the kitchen. Take whatever you need! When are we leaving for the hospital? How is Kristie? Where is Stacie? Is Kristie okay? Can I go now?"

During the entire duration of this interrogation with Detective Leonard, he was constantly being paged, his cell phone was ringing, officers were coming to the car to relay information, they were seeking directions, and the police radio was going non-stop. It was mass confusion.

After what seemed like hours but was actually only a few minutes, the detective flagged down an officer who escorted me back to the waiting cruiser that I was originally placed in. We walked back past our house, yet again I have no recollection of it.

When I climbed back into the back seat, everyone was there: Bobby, the chaplain, and the officer. We sat and waited again. I asked what we were still waiting for. The officer responded, "Clearance." I lost all composure at that point.

Screaming, I shouted, "This is not an 'explicit' airplane. You put the car into drive, press the gas pedal, and go!"

He immediately radioed his commanding officer and was advised he could proceed to the hospital. *What kind of morons am I dealing with here?* I was frustrated beyond frustrated. But I also had no idea as to the protocol that needed to be followed. I was thrust into total darkness, which resulted in horrific shock, denial, and grief beyond comprehension to humanity. I needed answers, and I desperately needed to get to Kristie, whether she was dead or alive.

## Chapter 10
# Where's My Daughter?

*"The people walking in darkness have seen a great light;*
*On those living in the land of the shadow of death a light has*
*dawned."*
Isaiah 9:2 (ESV)

Finally, the car was moving. My anticipation and perception of an emergency involved lights and sirens that would be blaring: This is an emergency! We would arrive in ten short minutes at the most.

However, there were no lights and sirens. There was no hurry on the part of the officer driving the vehicle. He was going home to his family tonight. We drove fifty miles per hour in a fifty-five mile per hour speed limit on the interstate while the conversation between the officer and the chaplain continued as two long lost friends catching up.

I continued demanding to know why we were driving so slowly! I was ignored. We weren't told anything about the hospital or Kristie's status. We were not privy to any information. The slow drive was excruciating! I was climbing the walls of insanity.

Twenty-five minutes later, the hospital entrance was directly ahead. We were almost there. I was ecstatic and hopeful of finding someone who would help us find my daughter. I expected to be dropped off at the front door and be rid of Barney Fife and his comrade.

\Instead we turned off the main road before reaching the entrance to the hospital. "Where are we going?" I demanded to know. The officer said he needed to park. "Park? Why? Take us to the front entrance!" Instead he drove into a large faintly lighted parking lot and drove to the farthest parking spot from the building as possible. He even backed the car in, as if he may have to leave unexpectedly. And there we sat and waited while he cleared his location with dispatch. I was fuming and about ready to blow my top! I tried to open my door, and, of course, it was locked. I don't recall any words that I probably said out loud, but I'm positive they were not nice.

Eventually the officer and chaplain stepped out of the car, and after pounding on my door in an attempt to thrust it open, the chaplain opened my door. Bobby had to wait for the officer to open his. I stood and anxiously waited for them to take the lead. They stood there with an uncertain look as to where to go. I was trying hard to be patient, but inside I was exploding. I looked toward the building and saw a man dressed in a white lab coat exit through a back door. It appeared to be an employee entrance. I took off toward the door. Everyone followed me.

We entered and stopped. Standing there inside the door, I expected the officer or chaplain to take the lead at that point. We all just stood there, looking at each other. Trying to figure out what to do next, I glanced down the hallway. My perception of that hallway was a very long, long narrow hallway, completely deserted and extremely narrow and closing in as I stood there anticipating what to do next.

I was in shock without realizing it, and everything was distorted. I saw what appeared to be a person, walking toward us, and I began to quickly walk toward her. As we approached each other, a lady came into focus -- a woman dressed in white, maybe a nurse. Finally, we met, and I asked her if she would help me find my daughter. She swept past me and continued walking as if I were invisible. She never acknowledged us, never paused, or never made eye contact with us. She kept on walking and left the building. I stood there dumbfounded. With all eyes on me, I turned and headed in the direction from which she had come, furious with everyone, and determined to find my daughter!

We trekked for what seemed like miles through the back halls of the hospital and finally reached a reception area. Finding an information desk, I stood in line and waited, and waited, and waited. Everything moved in slow motion. When I reached the receptionist, I was talking so fast she couldn't understand me. No one in my party came to assist me. I tried three times to explain that my daughter was brought to the hospital by Air-Care from Manassas around 5:00 p.m. Eventually, understanding I needed assistance with a surgery patient, she calmly replied "Honey, you need to go to the information desk over there (pointing across the lobby). That is the check-in desk for surgery patients. This desk is for doctor appointments."

I didn't want to stand in another line; I needed help. She had no idea what I'd been through or what it took to get there. I needed *her* to help me *now*. I didn't want to be passed off to another receptionist. Frustrated, I explained again, and again she reiterated she could not help me. Confused, dazed, in shock, frustrated, and at my breaking point, I looked across the enormous lobby in the direction she was pointing to find another receptionist sitting at a desk with a very long line before her.

I found my way to the information desk and waited. While standing in the long line, I noticed this teenage girl sitting behind the desk with an attitude a mile long, popping gum, and tapping her fingernails. When I reached her, she didn't speak but sat looking disgusted that I interrupted her. I calmly stated my request, and she typed Kristie's name into her computer.

Without looking up and with an attitude that shouted, "I hate my job," she said, "We ain't got no patient by that name."

I spun around and looked at the officer; he looked at me with a puzzled look and immediately turned toward the door and radioed his commanding officer.

I turned back to the young girl and practically spit out the spelling of Kristie's first and last name, demanding she check again. She sighed heavily and checked again. "She ain't listed as a patient here." I advised her that I was told by Prince William police that Kristie had been flown there by Air-Care around 5:00 that evening. The officer walked over and confirmed she was brought here by Air-Care and asked for a manager, the smartest thing I had seen him do all evening.

The young woman got on the phone, and in a hushed voice with her back to us, spoke to someone. She informed us someone would be with us shortly as she asked to help the next person in line. I was dumbfounded that she brushed us off so quickly.

Shortly, a pleasant little woman approached us and apologized immediately. Thinking she was apologizing for the rude teenager, I readily accepted her apology. She said, "We are working on assigning a social worker to your family. However, we are in the middle of a shift change, and it could be anywhere from half an hour to forty-five minutes. Please have a seat in our waiting area, and someone will be with you as soon as possible."

I was *stunned! Speechless!* Have a seat? My daughter's fighting for her life, and she wants me to have a seat and wait for someone to help us? Why was this happening? Before I could respond, she was gone. I looked back at the young teenage receptionist and decided it wasn't worth going after her. I looked around for someone to help us, reluctant to leave the desk. God help us!

The chaplain came over and took me gently by the arm and led me over to some chairs. He said they were sending someone to assist us.

I couldn't sit; I didn't want to sit! I needed to find my daughter! Now! Not in half an hour or forty-five minutes. What was taking so long? It seemed like an eternity. I paced and paced, going back and forth to the receptionist, asking when the social worker would arrive. She ignored me. Families and patients carried on as if we didn't exist. In their world, we didn't. We were of no concern to them. They had their own problems. Again, we were isolated.

A young woman with long brown hair and a beautiful smile approached us and introduced herself as Donna Rotondo, the hospital's social worker. She said, "Kristie is here, and she's in surgery. She was flown in by Air-Care around 4:45 this evening. I'll take you there." Finally, we had a functioning human being.

We got into an elevator, and I asked her why I was told Kristie wasn't a patient there. She said, "Due to the circumstances, she's under an assumed name." I inquired what name she was under. She said, "Jane Doe."

My body went limp, and I fell against Bobby. I became

instantly ill. That was the breaking point, and I went hysterical! I screamed at her that my definition of Jane Doe is a person who is deceased, and you can't identify the victim. I pulled on the moving elevator doors, trying to pry them open. The officer and chaplain pulled me away. After exiting the elevator, we were all five directed into a very small dimly lit waiting room furnished with a small sofa, chair, and table with the curtains drawn and extremely confining.

Donna worked to calm me down and assured me Kristie was not deceased and that she was in surgery, and she would find out her status A.S.A.P., and she left.

The chaplain asked Bobby if he wanted to take a walk downstairs, and he readily agreed. He had not said a word to me since telling me about Stacie. The chaplain asked what I would like to eat. I couldn't think about food, much less eat. I wanted to throw up. I declined, and they left the room. I eagerly waited for Donna to return. The officer stepped out of the room to contact his boss. I opened the curtains, thinking it would give me a view to the outside world but instead opened into the hallway. There were no other windows. Claustrophobia was a new experience and very unpleasant.

I sat there completely alone, praying to God, "Please don't let Kristie die!"

Donna returned a short time later, "Kristie is still in surgery, and the trauma surgeon will be in as soon as he can to talk with you about her injuries."

Relief washed over me. Justifying my fear, I thought it wasn't as bad as everyone had made it out to be. *She's fine. They are just being cautious and making sure she's okay.* "Thank God! Thank God!" I kept repeating.

The chaplain and Bobby returned a while later with a hamburger and fries and set it down in front of me. I almost threw-up at the sight of it. I asked them to take it away. I couldn't stand the sight or smell of food. It was all I could do to sit there and wait. The chaplain kept urging me to eat something. I picked it up and threw it in the trash can.

Donna asked if I had spoken to my family. I filled her in on the conversation with my mom and sister. I looked for a phone, but there wasn't one in the waiting room. I needed to call my family and give them an update. I asked Donna where I could find a phone. She looked around puzzled, and said she would find one quickly. She returned a few minutes later with a phone.

I called my grandmother's number, not realizing I remembered the number. My mom picked up on the first ring, very distraught. As soon as she heard my voice, she started crying. She explained that after talking with me earlier, the family arrived at Nana's. She began to suspect something was up when the entire family arrived unannounced. I'm sure the look on everyone's face gave a clue something was terribly wrong. Mom said they told her, and she instantly went into hysterics.

My grandmother never got over losing her son, the youngest of four children. Even in my state of mind, I knew Nana couldn't handle receiving the news about Stacie and Kristie alone.

Mom also informed me she had called Fairfax Hospital and was told there was no patient by that name. She then called all the surrounding hospitals in the area and was told the same. She then called the sheriff's department, but they had no information to give her. She called the hospital again and asked to speak to the family but was told no family members were present.

I assured her Kristie was there, and she was in surgery. We were with Donna, our social worker. I didn't tell her until much later that Kristie was listed as Jane Doe.

I asked Donna for the phone number my mom could call to reach me. I advised Donna what Mom had encountered, attempting to locate Kristie and us. She gave us her personal pager number and straightened out the problem, so if no one answered the phone in our private waiting room, she or the other social workers on duty would immediately be paged.

Donna inquired about my family's plans to travel to Virginia from Texas. I advised her they were attempting to secure flights as soon as possible. Donna received a page and stepped out of the room momentarily. It turned out some very close friends were at the hospital and were trying to locate us. I didn't learn until months later that they were given our location, yet my mom was told Kristie was not a patient there, and none of her family members were at the hospital, and, yet, our friends walked in and were given our location. Ironic, since hours earlier they couldn't tell me she was at Fairfax Hospital.

A few years later, I was invited as a guest speaker to give a presentation at the Police Academy. During one of our breaks, a gentleman approached me and congratulated me on the presentation and the S.T.A.C.I.E. Foundation.

He said, "I was there that night, January 29, 1999. That day is burned in my memory as if it were yesterday." I looked at him, trying to place his face. He wasn't familiar to me.

He continued, "The Prince William County Police Department instituted a volunteer pilot program, partnering officers with chaplains. Chaplains assisted with death notifications. I signed up, thinking it would be great to get involved. There were no formal training classes on how to deal with victims of crimes. We were given an assignment, and off we went. It was my first day as a volunteer and had been in the car maybe fifteen minutes when the call was dispatched. I had no idea what I was getting myself into."

I just stared at him for the longest time.

"You were there that night? You're the police chaplain!"

He said. "Yes."

It must have been the look on my face, as what he had shared with me began to sink in. He threw up his hands in self-defense and started backing away from me. I hadn't realized I was walking toward him.

He said, "Ms. Reed, I am so sorry. I had no formal training on how to deal with victims of crimes. I was trying desperately to help, but in all my years as a chaplain, I had never encountered this kind of tragedy."

He said our case touched him deeply, and he'd prayed for us every day. He requested counseling due to the brutality of the case. Because of his request, the police department mandated a forty hour training policy for police chaplains prior to ever hitting the streets.

I told him I now shared the story of the chaplain in my training classes because of the lack of compassion we felt, as well as the disorganization of the officers. He said it needed to be told because no victim/survivor should be traumatized by those who are trained and equipped and there to help. Speaking with him was a huge step in reestablishing my faith and trust in the police department. I understood that sometimes you learn as you go, but at the expense of the victim's families was not acceptable.

I sincerely apologized for my actions, and he assured me I didn't owe him any apology. The police department owed us an apology, which we have received numerous times. I thanked him with all my heart for having the strength and the courage to talk to me that day. So many questions were answered and many wounds were healed.

Chapter 11
# The Media

*"And the LORD opened the mouth of the ass...."*
Numbers 22:28 (KJV)

Inova Fairfax Hospital is a Level One Trauma Unit in Fairfax, Virginia, where Kristie spent eight days in the Women and Children's Center. The first five days were in the intensive care unit.

Our private waiting room was located down the hall from ICU on the fifth floor of the unit. During the evening of January 29, 1999, we breathlessly waited in silent agonizing torture for news of Kristie as the seconds moved like hours.

The door to our private waiting room finally opened around 10:00 p.m. as three close friends walked in. Otis and Brenda were our closest friends. Behind them stood Danny! It took me a few seconds to register in my mind that I knew them. We were just as glad to see them as they were to see us. All they knew was what the media had reported.

Otis and Brenda's handicapped son, Travis, was completely devastated by the horrific news, and they, like everyone, wanted to support us as well as be with us. We welcomed them with open arms. Travis and Stacie were the same age, and Travis was like a brother.

Danny was the security officer at Parkside Middle School and knew every kid, and every kid knew Danny. Those students looked up to him with the utmost respect.

He was always on their level and giving them second, third, and fourth chances to make things right. He didn't like to carry out disciplinary actions. Although he had a tough exterior, inside he was gentle and compassionate. Mrs. Liebert, the school principal, always supported him and vice versa. The students knew they could always count on Mr. Lawray and only push him so far. Stacie was one of those students.

He was a father figure to most of those kids. Stacie and Danny had a special bond. While driving home from work, he received a call from his boss, Mrs. Liebert, regarding the tragedy of Stacie and her sister. He turned around and drove straight to the hospital. He arrived at the hospital, but they would not provide him with information. Danny noticed Detective Naverette and asked him to let the family know he was there. I am told we asked Detective Naverette to place Danny on the approved list of visitors. I don't recall any of this.

This wasn't the first time Danny had encountered a tragedy relating to one of his students. Alex disappeared in June of 1990 and was found the following day, tragically murdered. He knew without a doubt he needed to be with us.

Danny would play a very important role in our lives for the next eleven years. He knew the journey that lay ahead of us and the aftermath that would soon ensue. He had experience in dealing with the media, the justice system, and he knew full well the grief suffered by Alex's family. He immediately offered us his support and stepped into the role as our families' spokesperson and our protector with our sincerest appreciation.

The media with camera crews camped out in front of

the hospital for days, hoping to catch an exclusive story. All we wanted was to be left alone. The hospital staff advised us to park in the hospital parking garage in order to avoid them.

Everyone authorized to visit Kristie was given a yellow wrist band with specific information for quick re-entry into the hospital. With so many family members coming and going, it was much easier to get past security when you were being chased down by the media.

That Sunday evening Bobby and I encountered a reporter who knew my truck and had camped out in the parking garage. He wanted an interview and would not leave us alone. We refused to speak to him, but he just kept on. I thought Bobby was going to deck the guy. He followed us out of the parking garage and onto the interstate. I feared he would follow us home, but Bobby finally lost him. Some reporters are vultures, preying on people at their most vulnerable moments. It's pathetic. We got a small dose of celebrity status. I don't want it ever!

Chapter 12

# One Who Lights the
# Deepest Darkness

*"And the God of all grace, who called you to His eternal
glory, in Christ, after you have suffered a little while, will
Himself restore you and make you strong, firm and steadfast.
To Him be the power forever and ever."*
1 Peter 5:10, 11 (ESV)

Doctor Futterman, one of three trauma surgeons on
Kristie's trauma team, came into the waiting room a little
after 10:00 that evening. Everyone stepped out to give us
privacy. He assumed we had received information from the
police as to why she was there. He quickly realized from the
look on my face, we had no idea what had happened.

Dr. Futterman was appalled we had not been informed.
He apologized profusely and asked what we knew. I told him
what little we'd been told of Kristie's condition; she was in
surgery and was not expected to live. He gently and as
delicately as possible shared her life threatening injuries
and why she was immediately rushed into surgery.

She'd arrived via helicopter around 5:00 p.m. that
evening with the trauma team awaiting her arrival. He
advised us that Kristie was alert and responsive upon
arriving at the hospital, which was a good sign. However,
she was in severe shock and had lost a lot of blood. She was
immediately taken into surgery. He said Kristie had been

bound with shoestrings when she was found according to the medics.

Bobby was able to verify she was bound, and the medics had cut them off. He asked Bobby questions related to Kristie's injuries. He tried to explain and shared what little information he knew of finding the girls and calling 9-1-1.

Dr. Futterman said Kristie's upper body was severely bruised, and both her wrists had been cut. Those injuries were not from being tied up. Kristie had suffered two stab wounds to her abdomen that missed her aortic valve by millimeters, which, if struck, would have caused her to bleed to death.

The knife that was used to stab her was very large with a serrated edge. And since Kristie was so thin and petite, he suspected the knife penetrated her spinal cord, and some additional tests were needed to see if she was paralyzed.

His news ripped my heart out! I was not prepared to hear this, and I couldn't wrap my mind around this horrific news. Stacie was dead, and Kristie had been stabbed? Why? Who? Why would someone so brutally attack two young girls? The questions kept coming, but the answers were far and few between.

He explained that he had to make an incision to her abdomen from her sternum to her navel to determine what vital organs had been damaged. "However," he explained, "the only damage we found thus far was the knife nicked her small intestine, which miraculously only took three stitches."

Listening to the details of my daughter's brutal attack, I was trying desperately to hang on to my sanity. I was hanging by a very bare, thin thread, and it was about to break.

Dr. Futterman advised there was more he needed to tell me. I couldn't bear any more devastating news. How much worse could this possibly get. My mind was on overload and I was rapidly sinking into oblivion. The doctor stated Dr. Dwyer, another trauma surgeon on staff, was working on Kristie's throat and neck. I jumped up, and screamed, "Why? What happened to her neck?" He explained her neck was repeatedly slashed, likely with the same knife, which only slightly missed her jugular vein by centimeters.

Their initial thought was her esophagus and larynx had been cut, and she would likely never talk again.

"Will she ever walk and talk again?" I interrupted. I needed to know!

Dr. Dwyer's examination found no evidence of any damage, he explained, but she was immediately placed on a ventilator to assist with her breathing. Thinking he was done, I thanked him and asked when we could see Kristie. Doctor Futterman hesitated and looked away.

I suspected there was something he wasn't telling us. Finally he said they needed to perform a S.A.N.E. test on Kristie.

"S.A.N.E. test? Why? For what reason?" I wasn't prepared for what I was about to hear. Dr. Futterman said they suspected Kristie had been raped.

The ledge I had been hanging onto just crumbled beneath me. "NO!" I screamed! "NO!" I cried.

Doctor Futterman advised that Sue Brown, the Sexual Assault Nurse Examiner (S.A.N.E.) would come in and explain the process prior to performing the procedure. He shook our hands and offered his condolences regarding Stacie and told us to let him know if we needed anything.

Nurse Brown came in a short time later and explained the procedure. She said Kristie would not know the test was being performed, as she was still heavily sedated from the anesthesia. Once the test was complete, she would advise us of the results immediately.

Several minutes later, Nurse Brown confirmed the S.A.N.E. test was positive. Kristie had been raped! I couldn't believe what was happening to us. I began to sink deeper and deeper into despair and hopelessness.

Doctor Futterman came back in shortly thereafter and told us Kristie would be taken into recovery soon. Once she was in ICU, we could see her. The doctor said she would not look like our Kristie. I also was told the next twenty four hours were critical. She had lost a lot of blood and suffered a severe trauma. I couldn't catch my breath. That thread I was desperately clinging to had unraveled and one thin piece was keeping me from falling into that deep black pit that was waiting to swallow me up, never to see either of my daughters again. If I lost both of my daughters, I had no reason to live. I was numb, traumatized, in denial, and suffering horrendous shock.

Around 11:00 p.m., the doctor came back and said we could see Kristie. My mind said I was standing and walking to the door. My body didn't respond. I couldn't move. My heart raced, my body was quivering, and my head was swimming. What would my daughter look like? Would I recognize her?

Dr. Futterman asked if we needed time to compose ourselves. I said "NO!" Holding onto Bobby, we were escorted back to ICU. Standing just outside the double doors, anticipating what awaited us, I froze. We had waited all night to see Kristie, and, yet, I couldn't get past those double doors. I prayed, "Lord, please help me!"

Slowly we made our way down the hallway. An ICU nurse came over, gently took my hand, and slowly led me into Kristie's room. Her room was dimly lit by the lights from the machines that were attached to Kristie. My eyes wouldn't adjust or focus as I peered into the darkness that I was certain was about to swallow me up. I kept praying I would awaken from the nightmare that was plaguing my mind.

Subconsciously, I heard the machines beeping and swooshing, as they monitored her status and breathed for her.

Kristie's small frail body barely made a ripple in that huge hospital bed. I didn't want to believe it was her lying there. And then I saw her face. It was my daughter! I was overwhelmed and consumed by my emotions. I ran from the room. I made it to the locked double doors of ICU and collapsed against the wall. I was told I was wailing a horrible sound.

The nurse was directly behind me. She took me sternly by the shoulders and turned me to face her. "Ms. Reed," she said softly, "Kristie needs you now. You need to pull yourself together and go back in there." I still couldn't cry, and I desperately wanted to scream! The nurse said, "She needs to hear your voice. She needs you to hold her hand and speak comforting words to her."

I looked at her like she had lost her mind. "How am I supposed to do that? I can't function on my own, much less help her!"

The nurse continued to softly talk to me, assuring me I could do it.

I finally pulled myself together, and we walked back

into Kristie's room. I delicately took her small frail hand and sat there staring at her for the longest time. Her face was not disfigured. She looked anguished. The words wouldn't come. My heart was in my throat, and I was completely numb. I remember the television being on and muted. We were the top news story. They kept flashing the girls' school pictures from last year and the same picture of the man I was shown by the police asking me to identify that person. I couldn't stand to look at him, and I turned away. Who was that person, and why would he do this to my girls? My emotions were in turmoil. I didn't recognize the pain. The grief was endless.

I sat by my daughter's bedside that night praying and asking for Jesus to heal my daughter. Over and over again, I silently prayed. In the early morning hours, I was wide awake and sitting beside Kristie. The ICU ward was very quiet. Suddenly, there was a loud ringing noise. It startled both Bobby and me. I saw a nurse walk over to the end of the nurse's station, directly across from our room, and answer the phone.

Our eyes locked, and she said to the other party on the phone, "Okay, uh-huh, okay." Slamming the phone down, still looking directly at me, she yelled to me from behind the desk, "I just want you to know they caught him!"

I was shocked. Why was she yelling? What did she mean they caught him? Who? And then she was gone from my view. A short time later, I asked the other nurses about her, but no one knew who she was. Our attending nurse stated there was not a nurse on the ICU floor who matched her description. I know I did not imagine that woman or the phone call.

It dawned on me a few minutes later that the person

responsible for this must have been caught, but why did she stand behind the desk and yell over at us, instead of coming into our room and sharing the information privately? The entire ICU floor didn't need to hear her yelling over a desk. I was furious with her. Who was that woman, and how could she have been so insensitive?

So what if he was captured? It didn't bring Stacie back or change what happened to Kristie. How did that nurse know the phone call was related to us? None of it made any sense.

I sat there in the quiet and continued to pray. Around 4:00 in the morning, I felt a peaceful presence enter the room. I continued praying. I recognized His presence, and I felt the serene peace of the Lord Jesus Christ as He wrapped His arms around us. He said, "She is healed." I knew immediately Kristie was going to be okay.

Bobby went home around 7:00 a.m. to shower and change clothes. He was still wearing his work clothes and had blood on him from the girls. Even while Bobby was there with us, I felt so isolated and alone. I called my best friend, Lisa, waking her up. She'd not heard the news and was shocked to receive my call. Her mom had cancer, and Lisa was her care- giver, but she came to the hospital and stayed with me for a few hours.

After she arrived, Kristie regained consciousness. She looked terrified and did exactly what the nurses predicted she would do. She was in fight mode and trying to protect herself. She didn't know where she was, and she was scared. I calmed her down, assuring her she was safe. The nurses came rushing in immediately and checked her vitals. She tried to reach for her breathing tube, but her hands were tied to the bed. She didn't understand, and her eyes said it all. She was reliving the attack. Pleading to me with her eyes, she needed answers.

I explained why she was being restrained and kept reassuring her she was safe. He was in jail. After she calmed down, the nurse said she would untie her hands if she promised she wouldn't pull on anything. She blinked her eyes twice saying "yes." The nurse untied her hands, and she put the call button in her right hand and told her if she needed anything, to push the button. They would check on her every few minutes.

After the nurse left the room, Lisa and I were standing beside her, and she motioned she wanted to write something. I found paper and pen, put them in her hands, and she began to slowly write the words, "Mom, do you know. . . ?" She was so weak her hand drifted down the page, and she couldn't finish her thought. She slipped in and out of consciousness for a few minutes, and she'd write another word. ". . . that Stacie is. . . ." ". . . dead?"

My heart broke for her and for me. We had no idea what she knew about her attack or Stacie's. Kristie drifted back off to sleep. Lisa left a couple of hours later to take care of her mom. She was torn between staying with me and being with her mom. I was extremely grateful she could come even for the short visit.

Kristie slept the rest of the day and through the night. Kristie's attending night nurse asked if she could wash her hair. It was full of dried blood, which she washed out with hydrogen peroxide and shampoo, then combed it out. She said it would make her feel so much better, even if she was asleep. It was comforting to watch the nurses care for her with such love and compassion. They were extremely gentle and patient with all of us. I understand it's their job, but to us, it was above and beyond. It was heartfelt, and they were wonderful.

A few friends came by that evening to offer their support. Two Prince William County detectives stopped by to check on Kristie and to interview her, but because she was still heavily sedated and intubated, they spoke briefly with me and offered small tidbits of information regarding the case. They confirmed his capture and advised he was uncooperative, and due to the ongoing investigation, they couldn't discuss the case. They said they would come back Monday and check on Kristie and hopefully interview her then.

My family arrived around 8:00 p.m. Saturday evening. I was elated to see everyone. It was painful watching them grieve, and, yet, I still couldn't cry. I found the strength to share what little details I knew from the doctors and nurses.

My mom asked if I had contacted the girls' dad. I had not thought about contacting him. I knew he needed to be informed. I struggled with making the phone call. Our marriage had ended on a very sour note, and we'd not spoken for more than two years, so our relationship was very strained. I finally worked up the courage to make the call only to hear his wife on the other end who wanted to know why I was calling him. I got pretty nasty with her, and after delivering the tragic news to Tony, we got into a heated argument. I hung up without letting him know what hospital Kristie was in. Someone called him back to give him the information, and he said he would get there as soon as possible. He was coming from Arkansas.

That night I was completely alone with Kristie. The Ronald McDonald House opened their doors to all fourteen of my family members. I was comforted by all the prayers, the support, and the Lord's healing. Yet, watching my daughter lying in that bed, bandaged, bruised, swollen, and attached to many machines while countless medications were being pumped into her damaged body, was incomprehensible. I felt that I had failed my daughters.

Sunday morning arrived, and I was anxiously waiting for my mom and sisters to arrive. I needed them with me and their support. I became overwhelmed with a huge wave of anxiety and grief. The reality of Stacie's death and Kristie's attack was setting in. The walls of rage and anger were building quickly as the shock began to wear off. The dam was about to break.

I paced the floor outside Kristie's ICU ward, around the nurse's station, and kept walking to the elevators looking for family members, repeatedly. I needed them at that very moment. I needed to know they were really there, that I had not imagined them. I also desperately wanted to get a shower and change into clean clothes. I still had on the same clothes from Friday morning.

The nurses were well aware of what was going on with me and asked if they could call someone. They offered to loan me clothes, buy me a meal, and sit and talk. They assured me Kristie was resting comfortably. I didn't have the phone number to the Ronald McDonald House and didn't want to bother my family; they would be there as soon as they could. I declined all the nurses' offers and continued to pace the floor, trying to avoid them and not interfere with their patient care as much as possible.

I couldn't sit still; pacing wasn't helping. I wanted to scream, get angry, and punch something until all the rage was gone. I wanted desperately to cry. I was at a breaking point. I was afraid I couldn't control it much longer. I was teetering on the ledge.

Finally, around 10:00 a.m., my sister, Theresa, stepped off the elevator, and there I stood with a look of panic on my face. She rushed to me, wrapped her arms around me, and I completely lost it! My mom and younger sister, Dannene, were directly behind her. They thought Kristie had died. I finally gave into my despair and crumpled to the floor wrapped in my sister's arms.

She held onto me while they ran to Kristie's room to check on her. Everything came crashing down on me, and I couldn't hold back the pain any longer. I cried so hard I was convulsing. The dam of my pent up emotions broke. All the pain and suffering came pouring out. Reality hit me like a ton of bricks, and the wall came crashing down. Theresa and I sat in the middle of the floor in front of the elevator for a long while.

Eventually Mom and Dannene came to check on me and let Theresa know Kristie was okay. They realized I wasn't. Our nurse said the doctor could give me some medication to help calm my nerves, but I declined. I have severe allergic reactions to medications, and besides, it just was not an option for me. I needed my mind clear and to be there for Kristie with my sanity intact. Nothing was going to get in the way.

Later that day, the doctor came in for his daily visit. He heard about my meltdown and again offered to give me a sedative. I refused. Kristie was awake and was taking everything in. He explained to her that her mom was fine and just needed to vent. Dr. Futterman advised Kristie was breathing on her own, and they removed the breathing tube. He said her throat would be pretty sore, and she shouldn't try to speak for the rest of the day. The doctor advised us to make sure we kept her calm and let her rest. The nurses didn't put any restrictions on the number of family allowed in her room, as long as we were quiet and didn't disturb the other patients.

On Sunday afternoon, the detectives returned to interview Kristie. We could not be present during her interview. I was not happy about that. She was interviewed as we stood outside her door. It was very difficult not knowing what she was going through behind those closed doors.

Donna, our social worker, asked me for the names of our close friends who we wanted added to the visitation list, so they didn't have to bother me each time someone showed up, and it wouldn't tie up the receptionist. I gave her the names of about ten friends. It was her way of distracting me, and it worked.

That evening a few of those close friends came to the hospital to visit. Our family and friends were standing in a large circle, about twenty-five to thirty of us, praying. Each one said a prayer.

Just as we finished, my youngest sister, Wendy, who had been sitting with Kristie, came running into the hallway. The look on her face scared me to death. All she got out was "Lorraine."

I panicked and fled to Kristie's room, thinking something was terribly wrong. I barged in, landed at her side, grabbed her hand, and yelled, "Oh my God, what's wrong?" with tears in my eyes and shaking. I scared her to death.

Kristie said, "Mom?" I didn't realize she had spoken to me.

Wendy said, "This is what I was trying to tell you!"

I said, "Tell me what?"

"She spoke!" Wendy said.

"What, you spoke?" I asked looking at Kristie. Her voice was very low and scratchy, but she'd spoken to me. She looked at me like I had lost my mind. I was so excited. Praise God, He heard and answered our prayers. Our prayer group was standing at the door smiling and crying. It was very emotional.

On Sunday evening after Kristie was settled back in and all our friends left, Bobby agreed to take me home, so I could retrieve clean clothes. Friends offered to go to the house for me, but I needed to go myself. Knowing in my mind what I wanted to do, going home briefly and looking over the house was far from what I actually thought I'd be able to do.

When we arrived at the house around 10:00 p.m., I discovered the girls' friends were having a candlelight vigil in Stacie and Kristie's honor. There were so many kids. I jumped out of the car and ran to the front porch. They all started hugging us, and everyone was crying. I was not prepared for that.

Eventually, I left the group and went to the back door. Could I possibly enter my house? I wasn't sure I could step over the threshold. Bobby unlocked the back door and stood there waiting on me. I couldn't move. It was very cold outside, and, yet, I couldn't make myself go in. I had been over that moment in my mind countless times when sleep eluded me. There I was, standing outside the door, dreading what I would find yet anxious to walk the rooms and hallways my girls had walked upon arriving home, wondering what I would encounter. Bobby put his arm around me, and we walked in together. He had turned all the lights on, but the moment I stepped into the house, something sucked the breath right out of me. I couldn't breathe or move.

Bobby recognized I was having a panic attack and talked me through it. We went downstairs, and I grabbed clothes. I had no idea what I had; then I threw toiletries into a bag and ran for the door. I couldn't get out of there fast enough. I got in the car and locked the doors. Bobby was still in the house. It shook me to my core.

My family stayed with Kristie while we were gone and worried about me. I shared the experience with them after we returned. We talked about what going home had done to me. I was unnerved, shaken, distraught, and extremely angry. Evil blatantly walked into my house and tried to destroy our family. What right did he have to rip Stacie out of our lives? I wanted to rip him to pieces. We decided the best thing was for me to try and rest, so I went to the Ronald McDonald House with my sisters, while Mom stayed with Kristie. Bobby went back home to spend the night, I had no idea he planned to return to work the following morning.

I didn't sleep at all that night either. It would be years before I would get a peaceful night's sleep. My doctor advised me to get melatonin to help me sleep; it didn't work either. The nightmares were horrendous.

On Monday morning, the doctors came in with the MRI results from the two stab wounds to her abdomen, which proved her spinal cord had not been touched. The good news kept coming.

Her throat and esophagus had not sustained any damage, but her neck was severely slashed, which took sixty stitches to sew it up. She was not out of the woods yet; she had suffered severe trauma and would be carefully monitored. She would have extensive scarring on her neck and abdomen, and physical therapy would follow. Dr. Futterman said, "She's a miracle." We all agreed. I knew without a doubt, Kristie was healed. The doctors weren't convinced as of yet.

Dr. Futterman asked Kristie to sit on the side of the bed. They took it very slowly. She sat up and was instantly dizzy and nauseous; however, she didn't complain but complied with the doctor's and nurse's requests. She was getting stronger daily.

On Tuesday morning, they had her up and out of bed. She walked to the restroom, and by Tuesday evening, she was walking around the ICU nurses' station with a walker and her IV pole. The doctors were amazed at her recovery. We knew that the Lord had laid His hands upon her. He had special plans for Kristie.

There were so many wonderful people praying for us, and from those prayers, we watched her progress rapidly. But we knew we still had a very long road ahead of us. Thank God we didn't know what awaited us in the coming days, months, and years. It was one moment by moment and one step at a time.

The hospital staff were truly amazing at every level. We were protected and cared for as if we were the only patients in the entire hospital that week. Kristie's doctors and nurses were attentive, caring, and deeply compassionate. They became like family.

The hospital staff members found something inspiring about Kristie. Donna, our angel/social worker, shared some very special news with us that Inova Fairfax Hospital Emergency Department's Trauma Foundation Fund donated $3,000.00 to help defray travel expenses for our family who traveled from out of state to be with us and attend Stacie's funeral.

We were truly blessed by so many wonderful and caring people who supported us through a very dark time *Thank You!*

On Monday evening, I received word that Tony, the girls' dad, had arrived, and I went into attack mode. I was not going to allow him back into our lives and start dictating after leaving us. Honestly, I was still very angry at him over our divorce and had never dealt with it. I vented my rage toward him. Attacking him justified my anger over the girls being attacked even if it wasn't his fault.

I needed someone to lash out at, and unfortunately, he caught the brunt of it. As soon as he got off the elevator, I was there and in his face. I verbally attacked him and caused a big scene in the main lobby of the fifth floor. Someone pulled me off of him. I physically attacked him and threatened him if he so much as upset Kristie. I would give no thoughts to his feelings or emotions.

When Tony walked into Kristie's ICU room, she was awake and faintly smiled at her dad. They embraced, and he cried. I stood in the doorway watching over her. I don't know what I expected him to do wrong. He was very protective of her as a father should be. But I was on high alert and watched every move he made. He grieved Stacie's death and Kristie's attack, but I had nothing to offer him. A few days later, I did offer a weak apology to him, but it wasn't heart felt. He was there for a week and we barely spoke to each other.

## Chapter 13
# The Morgue?

*"I tell you the truth, whoever hears my word has eternal life and will not be condemned; he has crossed over from death to eternal life."*
John 5:24 (ESV)

On Wednesday evening, February 3, 1999, Kristie was moved from ICU to a private room. While we were waiting for her move, I received a visit from a pastor whose church had taken up a collection for our family. We sat down to talk, but my mind was not on the conversation. I had a million things running through my head, until I heard him say "funeral."

"Excuse me, what about a funeral?"

He said, "I know you will need to plan a funeral for Stacie. . . ." I never heard the rest of his sentence. Those words hit me like a ton of bricks. I was shocked and mortified that I had not thought anything about burying my daughter or planning her funeral. I suddenly realized *I* needed to make her arrangements. How do I plan a funeral for my daughter? I had no idea since I had never planned a funeral before. The grief came in torrents of anguish and nausea; fear gripped my entire body. I couldn't breathe. I couldn't move. She was really gone! I hadn't accepted this fact but now was thrust into the reality of having to accept Stacie was no longer alive. I wailed. I couldn't accept her death for a long time.

The pastor prayed for us, and I was overcome with peace, a peace in knowing that I was not alone. The fear and anxiety was gone. I stood up and walked over to my mom and calmly said, "I have to plan a funeral for Stacie." She hugged me, and we cried as other family members joined us.

That evening Kristie was moved to a private room, and it took several trips to move all her belongings. She'd been sent cards, flowers, letters, stuffed animals, and balloons from all over the United States. I spent the night with her only dozing off and on. My body wouldn't rest, and sleep was still not an option. I sat quietly by her bedside, watching her sleep. She was still on heavy medication to help her rest and heal.

The next morning I announced I was going to the morgue to see Stacie's body. I needed to know in my own mind she was truly dead. I needed to see my daughter, and I had a funeral to plan. How do you do that? My family lovingly tried to talk me out of going, but I knew what I needed to do, and I needed them to understand why this was important to me. The scene in my mind of dropping Stacie off at school that Friday morning kept replaying in my mind. I was back at the high school dropping her off; she was walking away, turning to look back over her shoulder and smiling, while waving goodbye to me -- saying a final goodbye.

I needed to see her, hold her, and talk to her. I couldn't fathom that she was gone, ripped from our lives. My mind couldn't grasp the fact that we would never see Stacie again, hear her laughter, or see her beautiful smile. On the outside, I was emotionless. On the inside, I was screaming!

Bobby arrived at the hospital that morning to drive me

to the morgue. It was a cold and blustery day, and the drive from Fairfax to Manassas seemed like everything was moving in slow motion. I couldn't believe she was gone. I wanted to rewind my day and go back to those few precious moments with my daughters before the terrible nightmare started.

I prayed as I struggled with what I was about to do and what lay before me, but I needed to see Stacie. I reflected on her life of the past sixteen years and how I had almost ended my pregnancy.

I was nineteen years old and had recently ended a short- lived relationship with my boyfriend after learning he had cheated on me with his former wife. I moved home from Missouri and then discovered I was pregnant. Ashamed, I finally told my mom. She asked me to schedule a doctor's visit. I refused. I was sick for two months and not able to keep anything down and was terrified of seeing a doctor.

I finally called the Father regarding the pregnancy. He denied it was his and said that he couldn't have kids. I decided to abort the pregnancy. I could not be responsible for a child. I didn't want to be a single Mother, nor was I ready to be a Mom. I didn't have a lot of confidence in myself. I was extremely shy and introverted. The pregnancy only added to my dilemma.

I told my mom about my decision. She was adamant I would not have an abortion; she would adopt the baby and raise it herself. "No," I told her, "That's not an option."

I learned a few weeks later my aunt and uncle were expecting their third child. They had two red-headed boys, and this time they were hoping for a girl.

My uncle, Ernest, lost two children. His first born son Lyle, age seven and a half months, died from SIDS. My uncle remarried, and his wife had a daughter, Melody, who was a beautiful little girl with deep red, long hair. She fit right in with Ernest's other children. Tragically, Melody, at age four was killed when her mother accidently backed over her. My relationship with my aunt and uncle played a huge role in my life, and it was through their third pregnancy and support that the Lord gave me the strength to go through with mine. I would not be alone in my journey, and I had a very supportive family. I knew they would be there. I decided I could not have an abortion. Thank God for each member of my family. They ultimately changed the fate of my life, as well as Stacie's.

During my first trimester, I was hospitalized for four days due to severe dehydration. I had a dream the baby was a boy, and my son would have red hair. I would name him after my Uncle Ricky.

Nana, my maternal grandmother, was also a homicide survivor, having lost her youngest son, Ricky, and his girlfriend, Nita, July 26, 1969, to a drunk driver; both were age sixteen. They were killed instantly! Nana and I now shared a common bond.

My aunt delivered her youngest son, Ricky Lynn, in June 1982. He had red hair. This was the boy I had dreamed about. Stacie was born two months later in August 1982. I loved my uncle Ricky, and Stacie carried his middle name. Ricky was our legacy. Little did I know the legacy Stacie would leave at such a young age.

My thoughts were diverted to the kids at Kristie's school. What must they be thinking and feeling about all this? What about the parents, who must be mortified. The information I had received from friends and the media was that the school had called in counselors to help the students cope with the tragedy. They received daily updates on Kristie's status. Her progress was positive. So many people were praying for us.

The thought of so many kids going home to empty homes, as Stacie and Kristie had done, overwhelmed me. How were the parents dealing with knowing their kids we're going home alone? I turned to Bobby and said we need to go the middle school first before we go to the morgue. He didn't question me but drove to the school.

We entered through the elementary doors and walked to the office. The staff was surprised to see us. Dr. Bowe-Quick, the principal, was notified, and we were ushered into her office.

The staff assumed we came with bad news regarding Kristie. Upon hearing this, I immediately calmed their fears and shared that she was doing very well and making great progress. I said I needed to know how the kids were dealing with the tragedy.

Dr. Bowe-Quick said our timing was perfect; the media had been escorted from the building through the middle school doors. The entrances were on the same side but opposite ends of the building. They were there to interview the students in hopes of obtaining information about us. The school sternly advised the media they were not privileged to discuss the matter with them. The kids were traumatized enough and under the school's protection.

The Lord's timing is always perfect. He sent us to the school, protecting us from the predators prowling around looking for victims and the students from the snares of the media. He knew we needed to be there as much as those students needed us there.

I shared with Dr. Bowe-Quick that I was actually on my

way to the morgue but the Lord said to go to the middle school. I asked if I could speak to the sixth, seventh, and eighth graders. They called an assembly. Danny (the security officer at the school) was working when we arrived. We hadn't told anyone we were coming obviously, because we didn't even know until the last minute. He introduced me, but the kids knew who I was. Most of them had hung out at our house. As they filed into the auditorium, word spread quickly to those who didn't know me.

They were excited to be called out of class unexpectedly. The teachers greeted us graciously and seemed glad just to see us.

My heart broke as I looked into the faces of so many young children and saw the fear and worry that what had happened to Stacie and Kristie could possibly happen to them.

Although I didn't have a clue what I was going to talk about, the words came naturally, and we spent more than two hours sharing what had happened to the girls as delicately as possible.

The media had already given graphic, as well as false, information about us and the tragedy. I needed them to hear the truth and hear it from me as Stacie and Kristie's mom. I needed them to know how Kristie was doing, as much as they needed to hear about her progress.

Speaking from a mother's heart to the hearts and minds of those precious young children, I spoke about staying positive, focusing on healing, talking to each other, and not stuffing negative feelings inside.

"Don't allow your problems to escalate. If you feel threatened or afraid, or if someone makes you feel uncomfortable, please talk to your parents or a trusted adult about how you feel. Express your concerns and fears. Don't let anyone have power over you that makes you feel pressured, coerced, or a victim of circumstance."

This tragedy affected them as much as it affected us. I wanted them to know we cared, the community cared, and if they were struggling with a fear or an issue, it was okay to talk about it. They didn't need permission. It was their freedom to seek help and get answers.

I opened it up for questions, and they asked really good ones. "How did he get in your house?" "Did you know him?" "Did you like him?" "Was he a mean person?" "Did Stacie like him?" They wanted details of what happened to Stacie and Kristie. I was honest and careful sharing information, although I didn't have a lot to tell, but it was enough to satisfy them.

Someone asked if they could visit Kristie. I got so excited and without thinking said, "Sure, she would love that!" After talking for more than two hours, I thought to myself, *I would really like to give these kids a hug. But we're talking about sixth, seventh, and eighth graders. Kristie said it wasn't cool for eighth graders to be seen being dropped off at school by their parents, so how can I ask these kids for a hug?*

The Lord worked it out perfectly. I offered and stated I welcomed hugs, and if anyone in passing felt the same way, I would be standing at the door. If that was asking too much, especially from the cool guys, a *light* punch in the arm would do just as well. Their response was laughter. It was music to my ears. I needed to hear those kids laugh. It brought tears to my eyes and still does each time I think about that special moment. I still hear their laughter! We were covered in special prayers that day, and God answered each one specifically. Each child stood in line to hug me as he/she walked out, with the exception of one young man, who came up to me, smiled a shy smile, and lightly punched me in the arm. I smiled back and said, "Thank you!"

I would love to know where these kids are today.

We left the school three hours later, and although I couldn't wait to share our amazing journey with Kristie, family, and friends, I had another stop to make: Osbourn Park High School and Captain Porter of the NJROTC program. I had a funeral to plan, and I needed help. We arrived and were escorted to his class without being announced.

We were greeted with gasps of surprise from the students and staff. I wasn't aware we were so well known. We were taken to an empty classroom and shared with Captain Porter and Master Sargent Patterson the details as we knew them, which again wasn't a lot of information. They, of course, asked how Kristie was doing, if the media was leaving us alone, and how we were coping. They readily and graciously gave us permission to bury Stacie in her NJROTC uniform, which I had brought with me. Before I could ask for their help, Master Sargent Patterson advised the students wanted to offer their services. Captain Porter said we were in good hands and not to worry. I wasn't worried. I had such a weight lifted off my shoulders and felt tremendous peace. I had no idea that her classmates would step up and honor Stacie with a full Military Funeral Honors.

Returning to the hospital later that day, we were immediately pulled aside by a hospital administrator who was very unhappy with us. We learned the hospital was inundated with hundreds of calls from parents wanting to know visitation hours for Kristie. I shrugged it off as no big deal. But to the hospital, it was a big deal. The hospital was still responsible for keeping her under tight security, and we had breached the protocol. It's not a good feeling when you're reprimanded by the hospital chief of staff and security commander. But they got over it quickly. This was about Kristie and those precious kids and what they needed.

That evening more than a hundred kids and parents arrived to offer their support. Kristie wasn't too happy with me either. Some were curious and just wanted a glimpse of her, but most were sincere. She wasn't ready for all the attention from everyone. Honestly, I hadn't stopped to think about how it would affect her or the hospital. She was still in shock, as we all were. But every kid who came brought a smile attached to a stuffed animal, a card, flowers, or balloons. It was truly a God moment. To witness such an outpouring of love and compassion was absolutely beautiful. They needed to see for themselves Kristie was going to be okay.

After visiting hours ended and Kristie was settled back in bed, I noticed a huge weight lifted from her shoulders. She had been worried what people would think about her. *She needed that reassurance as much as they did.* Everyone was praying for us.

I felt bad for the kids, and maybe it wasn't the right thing to do, but it actually helped Kristie to deal with things later to come, and unfortunately, she would endure this kind of attention for years.

The media mysteriously learned about our visit to the school. Danny gave a general interview of what transpired from our secret visit to keep them away from us.

Danny's visit the next evening brought some good news; the school received numerous phone calls and letters from relieved parents expressing their gratitude about our visit. The parents heard their children's fears and concerns.

The truth was God needed to deliver a message of hope to His children; we were merely His messengers. Besides, I received a bigger blessing from their laughter and hugs. It was a huge step for me since I wasn't one to do anything so bold.

Standing before those kids, God had given me a courage and strength I didn't know I possessed. With my heart on my sleeve, I had stood before those kids and openly shared my grief and suffering.

The amazing journey transformed my life for His glory and honor. Life is a journey -- it's up to each of us as to how we choose to live it. I chose to make it positive. The journey has been long, but the Lord has been by our side the entire time!

We never made it to the morgue.

## Chapter 14
# Saying Goodbye

*". . . for I am the Lord who heals you."* Exodus 15:26b
(ESV)

The morgue called the funeral home daily, inquiring when Stacie's body would be picked up. I needed to focus on Kristie's recovery before I could schedule Stacie's funeral. Mr. and Mrs. Price, funeral directors of Price Funeral, kept the people from the morgue off our backs as long as they could. Stacie's body was naturally processing, and the morgue was upset she was still in their possession.

I felt horrible having to delay Stacie's funeral, but Kristie was my main concern. Stacie was in God's hands, and Kristie was adamant she would attend her sister's funeral. Kristie needed to say goodbye as much as we did.

Kristie healed quickly in her physical recovery, and because no further complications arose, she was released the following Friday, February 5. Stacie's funeral was scheduled for Saturday, February 6.

Stacie had earned and saved enough money from her job at Popeye's Chicken to buy a letterman jacket. Kristie was a little jealous and couldn't wait to get to high school. There were a lot of great perks to being in high school. Once we learned Kristie was going to be released, we dropped off Stacie's jacket to have some additions added. I wanted Kristie to have it to wear to Stacie's funeral.

On Thursday, Bobby, Mom, and I went to the funeral home and made plans for Stacie's funeral. Picking out her casket almost pushed me over the edge that I had been teetering on for the past seven days. The girls and I were supposed to be picking out dresses for the military ball!

Stacie liked Kermit the Frog, and her favorite color was green. Her favorite saying was, *"It's not easy being green."* In Stacie's honor, we chose a lightly-tinted green casket. That was an excruciating day for us. Yet, there would be many more over the next twelve years.

Because the media was relentless and kept harassing us, I asked Danny to schedule a press conference for Friday morning. Anticipating Kristie's release from the hospital, they were like vultures waiting for their prey. I was not going to have them stalking us and showing up unexpectedly. I needed to protect Kristie.

We arrived at the Manassas City Police Station to a room full of media people and law enforcement officials from several surrounding cities and counties. I was overwhelmed, but I faced them head on. Danny introduced us, which whetted their appetites. They wanted details, but they didn't get what they came for.

Bobby stood beside me, holding my arm as I spoke. Quivering with emotion, I thanked the communities for all their support. The outreach we received was incredible.

"We will prevail. Justice will be served. When Powell goes, he has to face God. God's going to deal with this," I said. I spoke about five minutes, but it seemed like hours.

To stand before a group of people was far from normal for me. My close friends and family knew how extremely shy I was. Ever since I was a kid and even as an adult, I struggled with severe shyness.

That day I stood my ground. They had overstepped their bounds, and I was not going to stand down until I had my say. I demanded they back off and respect our family's privacy. Kristie needed time to heal as we slowly tried to put our lives back together. I would protect her at any cost.

I don't recall the questions they asked except for one in particular. As we were walking away from the podium, one female reporter sitting on the front row respectfully asked "How's Kristie doing?"

I stopped short, stood directly in front of her, and stared her down with fierce anger. How dare she ask me about Kristie! I had just told them with absolute authority to back off. And she had the audacity to ask me a question? I said, "She's doing fine." It wasn't so much what I said in response to her question, but how I answered her. I said it with vengeance.

She looked startled and leaned back in her chair as if I had slapped her. I realized after I said it how it must have sounded. The room was deadly quite. No one spoke to me afterward. They had invaded our privacy. I wanted them to know where I stood on that issue.

Danny went back to the podium and thanked everyone for coming out. Our family stood in the back of the room, holding onto me as I stood there trembling after realizing that I had stood before fifty plus reporters and law enforcement officials.

Friday evening Kristie was released from the hospital. We were granted permission to stay at the Ronald McDonald House next door provided there was room since Kristie was no longer a patient.

Packing up Kristie's room was a chore. She'd received hundreds of stuffed animals and dolls, tons of get well cards and letters, flowers, balloons, and trinkets. The outreach and support were amazing.

The Ronald McDonald House overflowed with fourteen family members who joined Bobby and me in welcoming Kristie to her new temporary home. We rejoiced in Kristie's recovery, knowing tomorrow we would lay Stacie to rest, a bitter sweet day for all of us.

After all the bags and boxes were carried into our room, Kristie decided we need to unpack them that evening. I was called to the front desk and found Troy Sloper there with Stacie's letter jacket. He had heard Stacie's funeral was scheduled for Saturday and decided to personally deliver it to Kristie. His timing was perfect! I asked if he would give it to Kristie personally. He beamed from head to toe! We found Kristie giving orders as to where she wanted certain things.

Troy came in and introduced himself to Kristie. He expressed his sincere sympathy and wished her a full recovery. He then pulled Stacie's jacket from behind his back and presented it to her with her name embroidered below Stacie's name on the left chest:

Stacie 2002

Kristie 2003

On the right sleeve, we had "Sisters Forever" embroidered inside two linked red hearts with an angel below them. Kristie had not cried since before her attack. When she saw Stacie's jacket, she buried her face in it and wept. Every one of us, including Troy, was crying for both her and Stacie, as well as with her. It was so hard to watch my daughter grieve for her sister, knowing tomorrow we would say our final goodbyes to Stacie.

That evening we all arrived at the funeral home around 5:00 p.m. The family had an hour to spend with Stacie before they opened the doors to the public. I'm certain the media was there, but they kept a very low profile and left us alone.

We were greeted by Mr. and Mrs. Price with open arms. I have never met two more compassionate and caring people as the Prices. They went above and beyond their typical duties and were so gracious to us.

Mrs. Price styled Stacie's hair, painted her finger nails, and applied her makeup. As they prepared us for viewing Stacie's body, my mind drifted back to her laughter, her smile, and her passion for life of the past sixteen short years we had with her. As Mr. Price opened the door, I caught a glimpse of Stacie lying in her casket, and it was more than I could handle. I turned and fell against the wall and wailed. It was so painful. My mom held me. and we cried together. I know it was painful for everyone, and we couldn't accept that she had been taken from us.

I wanted my daughter to rise up from that casket and say, "Just kidding, Mom." Stacie loved to make people laugh. We weren't laughing that night. She was gone, taken from us so brutally. Would we ever learn to live without her? Would Kristie ever really recover from the brutal attack she had suffered? Only time would tell.

We lingered at her casket for what seemed like a very short time, and Mr. Price asked if we were ready to accept the public? No, we weren't because that meant we had to share her with everyone else.

At 6:00 p.m. we opened the doors, and the public poured in. We greeted every person who came to say goodbye to Stacie and express his/her sincere empathy to us and our family. I don't remember much of that evening. My mom said about half way through the reception line, my knees buckled, likely the effects of the shock, grief, and exhaustion. I sat about ten minutes and was back beside Bobby and Kristie. Kristie sat in a wheelchair. After about an hour, she was done. She needed to focus elsewhere on her friends. She greatly appreciated everyone's sympathy, but she's a private person.

I distinctly remember Dr. Afsahi, Stacie and Kristie's orthodontist, standing to the side of the receiving line, head down, looking solemn. He came to offer a collection his office had taken up for us. Inside was cash, checks, and a statement that read "paid in full." Stacie was a couple of months away from completing her treatment. Dr. Afsahi said he received my call that Stacie had been murdered. I had no recollection of making a call to his office, and we were deeply touched by his visit. It's amazing what we remember. To this day I see him so vividly, standing there with tears in his eyes. Stacie's nickname was "Skittles" because she always liked the brightly colored rubber bands in her braces. Kristie was known as "Baby Skittles." Stacie had touched so many lives.

The receiving line went on for four hours. The allotted time was two hours, but kids just kept pouring in. I was touched by all the young men and women who came to pay their respects to our daughters. We didn't leave the funeral home until after 10:00 p.m., after receiving more than two hundred people who gave their respects. The majority of them I'd never met before.

It was Saturday morning. The day had come, and I was not prepared for burying my eldest daughter at the young age of sixteen. I was reliving every moment with her in my mind. Sleep had eluded me for the past nine days. Every time I attempted to close my eyes, the horrible scenes of her last day played on the stage of my mind. I couldn't close the curtain. *God help me.*

The ride to the church was almost too much for Kristie. She was still very weak. When we arrived at Tabernacle Baptist Church, the media surrounded the church, trying to get a shot of Kristie. They were relentless. We arrived in a large passenger van and parked so as to shield Kristie from their view. Due to her wheelchair, we had to use the front entrance and wheelchair ramp.

Family members surrounded her to protect her from the cameras until she was being wheeled into the church. Still the next day her picture was on the front page: Kristie being wheeled into the church by her dad, Tony Reed, wearing Stacie's letter jacket.

Pastor Zorbas said the church was packed to capacity with many more people standing and even blocking the doorway.

The media kept their distance since the cameras were not allowed in the church. Sitting through the service, I clung tightly to what Pastor Zorbas shared only days before, "Ms. Reed, did you know Stacie received Jesus Christ as her Lord and Savior?"

"No! I didn't know; she never told me. Praise our Lord!" I was surprised, yet what peace filled my soul. I was elated to hear my daughter chose to ask Jesus Christ into her heart.

On a trip back to the house a few days later, I found her *Bible.* I found passages she had marked and notes she had written, and in the front pages, she had marked the date she received it from Meme and Poppy: June 12, 1994. She included a note: "This Bible belongs to Stacie, if found please return - Phone number (501) 94-7828." She missed a digit, and luckily she never misplaced it. On that day, I left a note: "Date of death – January 29, 1999." It was excruciating to accept her death and the life sentence.

Her little pink *Bible* has come unbound and sits on my bookshelf in my office along with her stuffed animal, Kermit the Frog. I miss my daughter terribly, but I have such peace knowing she is with Jesus, and one day I will see her again.

Every once in a while, I feel her butterfly kisses and know she is present. We love you, Stacie.

Pastor Zorbas quoted from *The Prince William Journal* as he spoke to the mourners in the crowded church, many of them teenagers. "Use this occasion to draw together and strengthen and pray for her family."

Her Uncle Gary read a poem he wrote just for Stacie:

"Little Frog"
This tragedy which confronts
makes you wonder why.
She was so young and beautiful,
she did not have to die.
They say things happen
once in a blue moon.
It should not have been this,
she was taken too soon.
Somehow this all fits in with
our Lord's great plan.
It is with wisdom so great
it cannot be conceived by man.
She was so young and full of life.
She walked a rocky road,
she had known much strife.
It is with a heavy heart that
we must let her go.
She would want us to carry on,

this I know.
Stacie resides in the house of our Lord
right where she should be.
So on the next sunny day,
gaze into the heavens.
She'll be smiling down
standing next to Poppy.
Goodbye little frog.
I'll see you on the other side.
Love Uncle Gary

Gene Kidwell, former Principal of Parkside Middle School, sang, "You Will Never Walk Alone." He'd recently had surgery but wouldn't miss attending her funeral, no matter how weak he was. Her fellow cadets carried her flag-draped casket from the church.

People lined Sudley Road for miles, expressing their sympathy and saluting the hearse as we drove by. It was touching to see so many saying goodbye. A sheriff's deputy was quoted as saying, "The drive to the cemetery was the longest funeral procession in the history of Manassas."

Upon arriving at Stonewall Memorial Gardens, Kristie said she wanted to walk to the burial site. We were half way up the hill, and she stopped abruptly and squeezed my hand. My heart dropped to my feet. I feared it was too much too soon. I put my arm around her back and held her to me. She said, "Mom, I need to go back to the van."

"Hun, we can sit it out if you're not up to it."

She looked at me like I had lost my mind. She said, "No, I need to fix the bandage on my stomach; it's coming off, and I don't want it falling off in front of everyone. I'm wearing a dress!"

We slowly turned and went back to the van, climbed inside, and shut the doors. They wouldn't start without us. We fixed Kristie's bandage and together made the walk up to Stacie's grave site. Kristie had a really hard time sitting through Stacie's final eulogy for several reasons. She didn't like that so many people were staring at her. She was struggling with so many emotions and saying goodbye. The guilt of burying her older sister was difficult.

Physically, she was in pain from the stab wounds and surgery and was still very tender. She managed to get through it gracefully.

At the conclusion of Stacie's service, I was presented with her flag by the NJROTC Cadets as the bagpipes played "Amazing Grace." I felt like the mother of a war hero. Stacie is a hero to so many.

On February 6, 1999, we laid Stacie to rest. The Osbourn Park High School NJROTC Cadets honored their comrade, our family, and the community by showing their true colors. We are forever grateful for their tribute to our daughter and our family. By invitation, Bobby and I, accompanied by my mom and stepdad, attended the 6th Annual Military Ball in Stacie's honor.

It was bitter sweet. Stacie would have been very upset if we had missed the ball. We were seated at the captain's table, and off to the right, sat a small table with a single place setting and an empty chair.

Master Sergeant Patterson read, "As you entered the room, you may have noticed the small table set for one that is off on its own. It is reserved to honor our comrade, Cadet Reed. Her life was abruptly cut short on January 29, 1999. This table symbolizes she is with us this evening, here in spirit.

Although Cadet Reed never fought in battle, she was highly respected by her comrades. She fulfilled her duties with honor. We should never forget Cadet Reed whose desire was to answer our nation's call and serve the cause of freedom in a special way. We are ever mindful that the sweetness of enduring peace has always been tainted by the bitterness of personal sacrifice. We are compelled to never forget that while we enjoy our daily pleasures, there are others who have endured the agonies of pain, deprivation, and death.

We shall never forget January 29, 1999, or our fallen hero who perished without the chance to enlist to serve her country. Cadet Reed is with us in spirit this evening, and we honor her with this small table set for one. The empty chair symbolizes our loss. The white tablecloth symbolizes the purity of America. The single pink rose reminds us of the life of our fallen comrade, Cadet Reed, and the loved ones and friends who miss her each and every day."

An easel stood beside the small table draped with a white cloth. I had not paid any special attention to it until the ceremony when Master Sergeant removed the cloth and presented us with Stacie's Certificate of Completion. It was for the successful completion of one year of study in Navel Science conducted at the Osbourn Park High School, January 28, 1999.

In the top left corner was the Navy NJROTC Patch worn on the cadets' uniforms, along with the NJROTC pin, a single gold star, and her ribbons of achievements. In the other three corners, were three Fouled Anchors, worn on the Garrison Cap.

The next presentation was a huge honor to us. A

certificate along with a small folded Flag of the United States of America read

"This is to certify that the accompanying flag was flown over the United States Capitol on February 1, 1999.

This flag was flown for the Reed family at the request of Elizabeth B Letchworth, Majority Secretary of the United States Senate. Signed Alan M. Hantman, AIA Architect of the Capitol."

A woman sitting at our table presented me with a pin -- United States Navy Memorial Washington D.C. The Lone Sailor is the embodiment of all who serve or ever served in the Navy. Created by sculptor Stanley Bleifeld, the statue stands vigil on the granite world map at the Navy Memorial Plaza.

Stacie's dream of joining the Navy, becoming the first female Navy Seal, or serving her country was reached. That flag of the United States of America, in honor of my daughter, represented her hopes and dreams that reached the hearts of many people. She was honored that night by those whose lives she so deeply touched. Thank you for keeping her hopes and dreams alive. I'm very proud of her. She serves in God's army, and she serves with honor.

I am very proud of who my daughter was and is to me and her family. She accomplished many milestones in the short life God gave us with her. And on January 28, 1999, she successfully completed one year of Navel Science.

One day, sitting in the waiting room for her last doctor's appointment, Kristie asked, "Mom, how come you didn't have more children?" My heart broke when she said, "I'll never be an aunt." What can a mother say to that?

Many dreams were shattered by one person's jealousy, rage, and anger. So senseless and selfish were his actions.

Our community outreach was incredible and gracious. We received an abundance of food, donations, cards, letters and phone calls from people just letting us know they were praying for us. One young lady, Heather Melillo, a classmate of Stacie's, held bake sales and raised over five hundred dollars to help with the purchase of Stacie's headstone. I'm still deeply touched by her thoughtfulness.

The cemetery advised us to wait at least six months to a year before putting a headstone down in order that the ground would settle. It was difficult to visit the cemetery and not have a headstone for her. Six months later we ordered her headstone, as it would take several months to complete it. It reads Stacie Lynn Reed ~ August 21, 1982 ~ January 29, 1999 NJROTC "One of the Elite" with a frog in one corner and her photo in the other.

I remember driving the girls to the doctor's office, and our route took us by Stonewall Memorial Gardens. We always commented on how beautiful and peaceful it was. The tranquility, duck ponds, and beautiful rolling hills, with the Blue Ridge Mountains as a backdrop, was surrounded by the Manassas Battlefields. A few short months later, it would become Stacie's final resting place, all too soon.

Stacie and Kristie ages four and two. The girls liked to dress alike.

Stacie and Kristie with Nana.

Stacie, Kristie, and Mom in Dallas, Texas. Mom took the girls to see the childhood neighborhood.

Stacie auditioned for America's Funniest People in Pine Bluff, Arkansas, in her Hawaiian dress, grass skirt, coconut bra, and boots in 1996.

Kristie and Stacie dressed for church. Kristie was being her silly self.

Lorraine Whoberry

Playing Putt Putt golf on vacation in Burlington, NC,
April 1997.

The Reed's own a gold mine. Well, not really, but
everyone can dream.

Stacie at her sixteenth birthday party. She was so happy. I was very proud of her.

Lorraine Whoberry

Stacie's school picture for her freshman yearbook at Osbourn Park High School, October 1998. She had shaved her hair due to a bet with another classmate.

104

Stacie's letter jacket after Kristie's name was added. It was presented to Kristie the day she was released from the hospital. She wore it to the funeral.

Lorraine Whoberry

Front step memorial and well. A candlelight vigil was held January 31, 1999.

106

Chapter 15
# A Safe Haven

*"He will cover you with his feathers and under his wings you will find refuge; His faithfulness will be your shield and rampart."*
Psalm 91:4 (ESV)

The Ronald McDonald House was a blessing to our family who traveled from Texas, Arkansas, and Missouri. Fourteen family members were housed in five rooms during their visits.

After Stacie's funeral, our family returned home.

Since Kristie couldn't return home immediately, we were invited to stay for as long as we needed. We stayed another three weeks.

My mom stayed for several more weeks after Kristie was released from the hospital. The three of us shared Kristie's room, which was stuffed to the gills with get well gifts. It was a safe place.

The Northern Virginia Ronald McDonald House is a home-away-from-home for families of children treated in area hospitals. The house has eight bedrooms and common areas that include living rooms, a dining room, kitchens, a common food pantry, playrooms, TV rooms, and laundry facilities.

The outdoor courtyard has a patio, picnic area, playground, gardens, and a walking path. They offer shuttle service to and from the hospital. The program is supported by volunteers, staff, and the spontaneous interchange between resident families.

One evening upon signing in, we chatted with the receptionist. She was a full-time college student and volunteered in the evenings. She said her boyfriend was a pilot with Inova Fairfax Air-Care. She said she shared with him our story. He said he knew about the tragedy and was the pilot for the medical crew that flew the younger sister to Inova Fairfax Hospital but didn't have any information about her status.

She called us back up to the desk later that evening, and we were introduced to Steve, the flight pilot. It was a pleasure to thank him for the work he did and to give him a hug. He hugged Kristie, and she personally thanked him. He said he didn't normally see his patients after the initial meeting, and it was a blessing for him as well.

The weeks spent at RMH were spent learning to adjust to our new environment. Kristie was still under Dr. Dwyer's care and physical therapy for her neck to regain full mobility. He wanted her to walk as much as she could without overdoing it. Kristie was active before the attack, and so it came natural for her.

Kids are resilient and, when surrounded by a positive environment, can heal in record time. We had a huge support system, and we felt each and every prayer. We were and are still very blessed by all our prayer warriors! Thank you to all of you!

During Kristie's first week out of the hospital and in between doctors' visits we made short trips to Manassas from Fairfax.

She was excited to be out of the hospital and away from

the RMH, so we took small trips to help Kristie adjust to riding in the car again. She would get nauseous and oftentimes sick. The motion sickness would subside soon the doctor said and was quite normal after suffering the attack and such an extensive surgery.

Our first outing was driving around the neighborhood, but we avoided our street. Over the next few days, we drove by the house in the day time. That way, it didn't seem so scary and daunting to her. Eventually, she was ready to see the memorial on our front steps. It was covered in plastic, so the flowers and stuffed animals would last until Kristie could see it. She wouldn't let me get out of the truck and remove the plastic. So Bobby would remove it during the day if the forecast wasn't predicting rain.

On the next trip, we pulled into the driveway for a few moments and left. A couple of days later, we parked and walked around the house. We took baby steps to help her adjust and regain her strength to eventually walk back into the house. Each step she conquered was a victory for her.

We visited friends and walked around the mall. It was difficult because people recognized us everywhere we went. Kristie didn't like all the attention, and she'd get upset. People needed to reach out to let us know they cared and were praying. This was not our normal lifestyle, so having all that attention was hard to accept. Kristie missed her friends and the normal routine, so we paid another unexpected visit to Parkside Middle School. Some of her friends spotted us, and the next thing we knew, we were surrounded by kids. Someone had a camera, likely my mom, and pictures were taken with her friends, students, teachers, and staff, as well as family. Everyone, especially the kids, were laughing, crying, and hugging. It was a warm welcome back. They could touch her and talk to her in their environment. Although we interrupted their classes, not one teacher complained.

They really enjoyed our visit and the chance to escape the classroom. The visit was very healing for everyone. She was excited about returning to school, which helped her physical healing immensely.

Dr. Dwyer noticed a big change in her attitude and enthusiasm after her visit to school and was not surprised when Kristie asked about returning to school. He agreed to release her with a few stipulations after only four sessions with her physical therapist. If she felt it was too much or needed to rest, she needed to let us know, and he would extend her leave. She had only missed three weeks of school, which was amazing.

He advised her she was still very weak and needed to take things slow. Kristie's a lot like her mom; slow isn't in our nature. However, she tired very quickly and let us know when she had had enough.

Kristie returned to school after three weeks, but it was extremely hard to let her out of my sight. I asked if I could shadow her all day, but she wouldn't have it. The school agreed to monitor her and call me if she needed anything, and she agreed to let her teachers know. I always left a phone number where we could be reached and only received one or two calls to pick her up early.

Occasionally, she would have a bad day but not many, and she learned to work through them.

While Kristie was in school, Mom and I would spend a few hours at the house, doing laundry, moving a few things back home, while trying to find that normal again. Although Powell was in jail, it was still very difficult being in the house, and we only stayed long enough to do what we needed to do and then left.

Our dear family and friends had cleaned and scrubbed the house after the police finished processing the crime scene. Stacie's room was put back together, and the blood stain on Kristie's floor was gone. But the scene in our minds was painful, and the feeling of being in the house was unnerving. I wasn't feeling very positive about returning.

That was our home, and we decided he would not take anything else from us. He would not control our lives. Yet, there was fear that hung over us that we couldn't easily shake.

## Chapter 16
# The First Step of a
# Long Journey - Home...

*"When you walk, your steps will not be hampered; when
you run, you will not stumble."*
Proverbs 4:12 (ESV)

A journey of a thousand miles begins with a single step.
According to *Webster's Dictionary,* shock or PTSD (Post-
Traumatic Stress Disorder) *"is a very intense and distressing
experience that has a sudden and powerful effect on one's
emotions and physical reactions."* My body was reacting to a
horrific tragedy, and I struggled to make sense of it. Most of
the time, I was functioning on pure adrenaline.

When everyone leaves and you are left alone with your
grief and pain, it's a lonely place. Going home was very
unsettling to us. Home was a scary place for me, and I
couldn't imagine how Kristie would handle it.

Bobby had gone back to the house on Saturday
morning, the day after the girl's attack, and was spending his
nights there alone. I couldn't begin to imagine the demons
he was battling.

We were dealing with emotions that we couldn't
understand. We became strangers passing like two ships in
the darkness; we were lost, confused, and in complete denial
of this horrific tragedy, trying desperately to hang on and
make sense of all the horror. We were trying to pick-up the

shattered pieces and put our broken lives back together. The Monday following the girls' attacks, Bobby had returned to work.

Dear friends had come and cleaned the house and painted the entire upstairs, except for Stacie's room. Paint had been donated. Kristie's and Stacie's rooms had hardwood floors, one of the things that had sold us on the house. Kristie's room was painted in pastel colors. With Bobby being home to help orchestrate, all of this was a blessing.

We received a call from a furniture store, asking if Kristie would like to come down and pick out her new bedroom furniture. She was so excited; she didn't go to school that particular day. Although she went and picked out the furniture she wanted, she was given a full size brass bed, dresser, chest of drawers, and two matching night stands. We had decided to move her into my office a few days prior, as we knew she couldn't sleep in her bedroom again. There was plenty of room for her new bedroom suit that was soon to be delivered. We decided to make a trip to the house and actually walk in.

We knew it would be difficult for her, but she was determined she could do it. We arrived around ten that morning and sat in the driveway for a while before getting out of the car and walking around a bit. It was cold, so we made our way into the sun porch. It was the door we always used and the same entrance Kristie had made on January 29, 1999, when Powell opened the door for her on that tragic day.

I watched her to make sure she was okay. She struggled, and we told her to take her time. My mom had not yet been back inside either, so it was difficult for them both.

I had made a few trips back for clothes, but still was uncomfortable being in the house. It was now week two since Kristie's release from the hospital.

Kristie walked down the hallway, and we knew she was reliving every step, as she walked past her bedroom to Stacie's room. We all three gathered there and cried, hugged and prayed. It was another reality that Stacie would not be coming home to us ever again.

We left her room as it was. Her walls were a baby blue and green. The only thing done was the blood and broken mirror were cleaned up. Nothing else was changed.

Eventually Kristie got up the courage to walk over to her old room across the hallway. The door was closed. She slowly opened it and stood in the doorway of her old room, now my office. I don't know what she was expecting. I don't think she knew either, except to confirm Stacie wasn't still lying there on the floor. She looked down where Stacie's body had laid on the bloodstained floor I could see her reliving those fateful moments before her brutal attack. I cried for her, Stacie, and the pain I knew she was carrying in her heart.

Her new bedroom furniture wouldn't arrive until next week. Again, it was perfect timing. Each day we would return to the house and linger for a short amount of time, sometimes several times during the day. While Kristie was at school, Mom and I would visit the cemetery, go shopping, or visit friends, seldom going to the house.

One day, we had to do laundry and we couldn't stand the thought of going to a laundry mat. So we took our clothes home. This meant going into the basement to do laundry. None of us had had the nerve to venture to the basement on our trips to the house. Maybe the laundry mat wouldn't be so bad after all.

We didn't mention to Kristie that morning that we were going home to do laundry. We dropped her off at school and went to the house. Instead of carrying the laundry down the steps, we went down together first, unlocked, opened the basement door, and hurried outside. We carried the clothes into the basement from the back door.

It was too eerie just getting down the steps, let alone trying to carry the clothes, something I had done countless times before this horrible tragedy. I don't recall what we did while the clothes were washing and drying, but we got them done finally.

Stacie's laundry, that she had started the day the girls were attacked, including all our laundry, had been taken home by a neighbor and finished. What an act of true kindness. It was unnerving being in the basement where Kristie was so brutally attacked. I could envision her lying under our bicycles, bound, nude, and bleeding. I'm sure my mom was having the same vision I was having, and we couldn't get out of there quick enough.

The next week, we moved Kristie out of the Ronald McDonald House. We said goodbye to our friends whom we had shared lots of meals with during our stay. My fellow employees were dropping off three meals a day, and because there was so much food and only three of us, we were feeding anyone who could and wanted to eat; families of patients, volunteers, and staff. That included taking food to the firehouses, and donating lots of dry goods to the Ronald McDonald House. We had a great time getting to know the families, listening to their stories and their struggles, and sharing a common bond, grief and hope, from which came friendships.

It was difficult to say goodbye, but this part of our journey had come to an end, and it was time to move back home. Mom stayed several more weeks. I loved having her there just as much as Kristie did.

Since the attack, someone had been with Kristie all day long. Now we would encounter a new struggle. Kristie would not sleep by herself, and my mom slept with Kristie for the next several weeks. After Mom returned home, I slept with Kristie for the next six months. Kristie could not tolerate the dark or the quiet, so twenty four/seven the lights were on along with the television or radio. We compensated and did whatever it took to make her more comfortable and to feel safe.

We began receiving calls from various companies regarding donations. A carpet company called and asked when they could come and measure for the new carpet. "New carpet?" I asked Bobby if he ordered new carpet and forgot to tell me. He knew nothing about new carpet. I told the guy he had the wrong customer. He verified the order was for the Reed-Culver family. I asked who made the request, and that's when we learned the neighbors had asked them to donate new carpet. We were shocked.

Every day we would find gifts left on the porch. One family dropped off a comforter, with matching sheets. Kristie chose to have her room painted pastels of blue, green, yellow, and pink, with each wall painted a different color. Bobby made shelves and painted them the same color.

It was very comforting and peaceful walking into her new bedroom. The comforter and sheets matched perfectly, and the family who gave them had no way of knowing how perfect their gift was. Good moments were happening minute by minute. And the prayers were heartfelt.

Chapter 17
# OREO

*"My God is my rock, in whom I take refuge my shield and the horn of my salvation. He is my stronghold, my refuge and my savior— from violent people you save me."*
2 Samuel 22:3 (ESV)

We were deeply touched by the support of our friends, neighbors, and communities. After arriving back home, we felt we needed to express our gratitude to everyone for all their support. We placed a large banner in our yard to express our sincerest thanks. *"THANK YOU COMMUNITY!"*

The following day our banner appeared in the newspaper. We left it up for over a month until we received a nasty note in our mailbox, unsigned. It was very negative and said we needed to take that *(explicit)* sign down because it was a horrible reminder of what happened, and we needed to get over it and move on.

Get over it? Move on? We had just buried Stacie, and barely a month had gone by. What kind of idiot tells you to get over it and move on? People said we needed closure. What is closure? The only thing closed was the lid on Stacie's casket! We were mortified! The note left in the mailbox was negative, degrading, and nasty. I was not about to take down the banner, especially after receiving that letter!

The sender didn't have the courage to sign his/her name. That's a coward in my book. I would love to have had a face to face talk with that person to find out what exactly his/her problem was. Who were they to tell me it was time to get over the horrific tragedy we were still suffering? We were desperately trying to get through each day, second by second. The next day, Bobby took the sign down. I was furious.

The letter made us all very uncomfortable, let alone being back in the house.

Kristie asked if we could get a dog. We all needed a sense of security. I was thinking of a German Shepherd, a ferocious dog who would protect us. Bobby took Kristie to the pound and came home with a speckled, stubby legged, long round body, long ears, black and white spots, something of a dog, which sort of resembled a dwarfed Dalmatian. She named him Oreo. He was actually a Beagle and Australian Shepherd mix. He turned out to be a very lovable dog

As soon as Kristie saw him, she knew he was the one. He went right to her, climbed into her lap, and settled in for a long period of petting and love. The bond was instant. *So much for a guard dog; there is no way he will live up to our expectations,* I thought. *We have a scaredy-cat for a dog, afraid of his own shadow and* likely to run and hide at the first sign of trouble.

Oreo proved to be a good guard and watchdog. He had an instinctive, yet gentle nature and knew Kristie was fragile. He was very protective of her and never tried to hurt her or jump on her. Oreo and I would walk her to the bus stop every morning and pick her up every afternoon. He always knew when it was time to leave. If someone he didn't recognize tried to approach us, he was on guard, and you were not getting within fifty feet of either of us. If we didn't calm him down or call the person's name, the hair on the back of his neck stood up, and he bared his teeth unless we told him it was okay, and then they'd get licked to death. He proved to be a great guard dog, as well as really good pet.

But there were times I could have sent that dog packing. One afternoon Bobby was at work, and Kristie was at school. Mom and I were in the basement doing laundry, and we were talking. It was uncomfortable being in the basement. We were trying to hurry and get back upstairs. Suddenly, we heard someone walking across the dining room hardwood floor. We froze, ready to bolt for the back door but were paralyzed.

I called Bobby's name, thinking maybe he dropped by to check on us. There was no answer. And then we heard the sound of keys jangling. He wore a ring of keys on his belt. Why didn't he answer me? Mom and I both stood frozen with sheer panic on our faces. We were so scared. The back door was locked, and Oreo wasn't barking, so it had to be Bobby. We waited breathlessly at the sound of heavy work boots coming down the stairs.

Then, around the corner came Oreo. We both screamed, which sent him in a panic back upstairs. And we burst out laughing hysterically. We could have killed that crazy dog. His tags on his collar sounded like keys jangling. He had no clue he had scared us half to death. We looked everywhere for him, called his name, and finally found him under Kristie's bed, in the farthest corner, cowering. We got him out and loved on him, still laughing.

He was a lot of fun and was always doing something funny. Having him around eased a lot of tension and gave us a sense of security. He didn't sneak down to the basement for a long, long time. We also had two cats before we adopted Oreo. He always wanted to play with them, but they didn't care for him. He was a playful, loveable pup that wanted to feel loved. We believed he had been abused by a male figure the way he cowered around men. But he had Kristie, and Kristie had Oreo. He was loved.

A year later we adopted a yellow tabby kitten and named him Tuffy. He really thought he was tough and thought he was a dog instead of a cat. He soon took over Oreo's bed. Tuffy would stretch out, and Oreo would lay beside Tuffy with Oreo's arm laid over Tuffy's shoulder, and they would snuggle for hours. They were best buds.

One evening I was downstairs and heard Oreo barking ferociously. I ran upstairs and found Oreo in the kitchen. He had Markey, Kristie's friend, cornered up on the counter. I called Oreo off, but he was not leaving. I yelled for Kristie, who was right behind me. She called him off and grabbed his collar and dragged him away. He was not going to let Markey in.

Once we got Oreo away, I asked Markey what happened to set him off like that. He said he knocked at the door, and Kristie let him in. She left the kitchen, and suddenly Oreo was growling and trying to bite him, so he jumped up on the kitchen counter. We had to lock Oreo in the basement for a while. We never did figure out why he reacted that way. After that incident, he was fine with Markey being around as long as we called his name, and Oreo saw we were okay with him being there.

If anyone knocked on the door, we had to let him/her in and call him/her by name or else our fierce guard dog would try to eat him/her up. Our house was his territory, and he had staked his claim.

# Chapter 18
# Motions, Hearings and, Disappointments

*"As the old saying goes, from evildoers come evil deeds, so my hand will not touch you."*
1 Samuel 24:13 (ESV)

Paul Warner Powell was held on an outstanding warrant for contributing to the delinquency of minor charges from 1997. He was arraigned on Monday, February 1, 1999, in juvenile court without bond at the Prince William Adult Detention Center on charges of murder, rape, abduction, malicious wounding, grand larceny, and three firearm charges in connection with the attack of Stacie and Kristie. He was interrogated for hours and yet denied most of his involvement in the girls' attacks.

Detective Leonard had been assigned to the case and knew Powell from Officer Leonard's days as a truant officer. Powell was being taken to interrogation when he saw Detective Leonard walking down the hall. He told the officer in a smirking tone he would only talk to Detective Leonard!

Powell had told his roommate he needed to return a movie on January 28. He asked to borrow his car. When Powell didn't return the next day, his roommate and several of his friends went looking for him. They found the car parked at Prince William Hospital, less than four miles from our house, which they had reported stolen that morning.

The police were at Powell's Mom's house when the friends pulled up with the stolen car. His friends asked if Powell was there, and the officers asked why they were looking for him. When the police learned about the stolen car, they impounded the vehicle. A 9mm handgun was missing from the vehicle the owner told police. One young lady told the officers she knew some of his hangouts, so they drove her around in a police cruiser. Later that evening, she spotted him through a second story window in a townhouse.

The S.W.A.T. Team was called in and staked out the address. They learned Powell's friend's girlfriend and two young daughters lived there.

The S.W.A.T. Team waited for hours for movement. Finally, Powell's friend stepped out onto the porch to smoke a cigarette. The S.W.A.T. Team took him into custody. When he didn't return after several minutes, Powell stepped out onto the porch looking for his buddy. Before he could light a cigarette, the S.W.A.T. Team arrested him.

Powell was packing a bag to leave town. On his person, they found three knifes, including the one they suspected he used to stab the girls. Among many pieces of evidence, this would be crucial due to the girls' blood being on the knife and sheath.

Detective Leonard interviewed Powell for hours on end the night he was captured, yet Powell knew the system and only confessed to stabbing Stacie.

Powell would not confess to the attempted rape of Stacie or the rape of Kristie. Being a Friday night, Detective Leonard was able to interrogate him all weekend before he obtained an attorney.

After Powell's arraignment, Detective Leonard, accompanied by Jim Willett from the Prosecuting Attorney's office, visited us at the hospital and interviewed Kristie again regarding specific details as their key witness. He confirmed Powell's arrest.

After arriving back home six weeks after the attack, we received an introduction letter from the Commonwealth Attorney Victim Witness office introducing themselves. I wasn't knowledgeable of this organization and had no idea who they were or what they did. We weren't introduced to our Victim Witness personnel until I got to attend Powell's fourth hearing.

I had asked to be notified of the motions, hearings, and all other events, even if he were moved within the jail. I wanted to know where he was at all times. Kristie was terrified that he would possibly escape and come after her again since she had survived. We would learn during the trial that Powell wrote letters to his friends. He wanted them to kill Kristie, so she could not testify against him. They refused to carry out his requests and reported this to the prosecutor's office immediately, unbeknownst to us.

I adamantly expressed to Detective Leonard, the prosecuting attorney's office and the prosecutor, family, friends, and neighbors that I wanted to attend every motion and hearing because I wanted to make sure he saw my face and was constantly reminded of the horrible crimes he committed against my daughters and our family. We were pursuing the death penalty. We wanted him to suffer greatly. It was painful as we waited for hearings and motions to be scheduled, as well as notifications.

I received a call from a friend several months after his arraignment, asking how the hearing went. I had no idea what she was referring to.

She proceeded to tell me about an article in the paper

about a motion that was filed and that Powell had appeared in court. I was extremely upset because I had not been notified about any hearing. I knew nothing about the motion. I contacted the Prince William County CA's (Commonwealth Attorney's) office and spoke to the receptionist, advising I was not informed of Paul Powell's court date the previous day. She apologized and assured me this was an oversight. I would be contacted when the next hearing was scheduled.

I accepted her apology and waited for the next call. The next call came a few months later from another friend, inquiring if I had attended Powell's hearing the previous day. I scoffed that I knew nothing of that hearing, again. She advised me she had read about it in the local paper.

I called the CA's office again and asked to speak directly to Mr. Paul Ebert. We were connected after a long hold, and I informed him of the non-communication between his office and myself regarding the hearing the previous day involving Paul Powell. He apologized and said he would flag the file. We would be notified of the next hearing. I once again accepted his statement as carved in stone, straight from the horse's mouth.

A few months later on my way to work, I was sitting at a red light and glanced over at a newspaper stand to see his [Paul Powell] face on the front page of the paper. I made an illegal left turn from the opposite lane with two lanes of oncoming traffic, only to read there had been a hearing the previous day that I was not notified of. You can probably guess how angry I was after reading about it in the paper myself. I drove straight to the CA's office at seven-thirty in the morning and waited. The courthouse didn't open until 8:00 a.m.

As soon as the doors opened, I went straight to the CA's office and sat in the lobby for their office to open at 9:00 a.m. This gave me lots more time to build up more frustration. As soon as the office opened, I informed the receptionist, with a strong attitude, I was there to speak face to face with Mr. Paul Ebert. I was told he had not yet arrived, but I was welcome to sit and wait. I'm pretty certain he received a call regarding my visit before he arrived. I was not very happy.

I anxiously waited for more than an hour. I repeatedly asked the receptionist when he was expected to arrive. Apparently he had snuck in through a back door to avoid me and had been in his office for quite some time. I demanded to speak to Mr. Ebert face to face, and I wasn't leaving!

Shortly afterward Mr. Ebert came to the reception area and invited me back to his office. He was very cordial. I was fuming, and everyone knew it. As soon as we were in his office, I laid into him.

"Why was I not called about the hearing the day before? Why did I have to find out about it in the newspaper again? Why was I not informed like you promised? Did you forget to flag the file? Again? Why does your office have a problem picking up the phone to make a two minute phone call to inform me of a hearing?"

I'm sure everyone heard me yelling at him. Once I finally took a breath, he looked at me as if waiting for more questions. I glared at him to make sure he knew I was waiting for the answers.

Mr. Ebert looked at me and said, "Ms. Reed, we screwed up. And I sincerely apologize."

I'm not sure what I was expecting, but it wasn't an apology. He defused my temper immediately because it was truly heartfelt. He seemed to be a man of compassion. I responded by saying, "Well, what are you going to do about it?"

Mr. Ebert's response was, "Please excuse me one moment." I almost lost control. I thought he was putting me off and was ready to come unglued, but my spirit told me to sit tight. Instead, he called all of his staff associated with the Powell case to his office, including the Victim Witness Director, Patty Allue, and Detective Leonard. He advised me he was calling an emergency meeting, and they would all be there shortly.

A few moments later we were all gathered in his office. He introduced me to his staff, and advised every one of the situation. "We seem to have a communication problem in our office, and Ms. Reed has advised me of the issue. He said, "Ms. Reed was promised she would be notified by our office of any hearings and motions in Mr. Powell's case. We have failed her, and I'm making it very clear to everyone here that this had better not happen again. I expect we will do better in our service to all those we serve."

Okay, so this man had clout. I received apologies from all those present with the promise I would be notified if Powell so much as breathed wrong. I was satisfied with what I felt we had accomplished, but as I left those present, time would tell just how efficient the meeting was.

Well, as it turned out days prior to the next hearing, I received fourteen phone calls in a two-hour time frame. Mr. Ebert, Mr. Willett, Mrs. Allue, and Detective Leonard contacted me personally regarding the hearing that was scheduled the next week in Powell's case. Okay, we got our point across, and I was continually informed of all future court dates in a timely manner, as well as countless courtesy calls from each of them, asking how we were doing, if we needed anything, and if we had any questions or concerns. Things were looking up in the communication process.

I attended the next hearing and waited anxiously for Powell to walk into the courtroom. Shortly after the judge entered, Powell was brought in. Our eyes locked for maybe a split second, and the moment he saw me, he quickly looked away and turned white as a ghost. He refused to look at me again. He was in handcuffs and shackles. I had no fear of him, but I had a lot of rage and anger toward him. During that first hearing I attended I was accompanied by Mrs. Allue from Victim Witness, Mr. Ebert, and Mr. Willett from the prosecutor's office. His defense attorneys were horrible in my opinion.

What really struck me was Powell's demeanor. He was so cocky and arrogant. He kept rocking back and forth in his chair. It was extremely aggravating to me. Seriously, I wanted to knock him out of that chair. His body was covered in tattoos (the parts you could see). On the back of his neck, was an eyeball. We were informed by Detective Leonard he was a self-proclaimed member of the Ku Klux Klan, as well as a white supremacist. I needed to know what drove him to brutally murder and attack my daughters.

Seeing him in person for the first time brought up a lot of anger I didn't know I possessed. I wanted him to die a very excruciating and painful death. I went home and shared with Kristie what had transpired. She said to me, "Mom, he's pure evil!" It made my blood boil.

Paul Powell had no idea who he was up against! And I pledged he would die at the hands of the state or the hands of other inmates. And I vowed to become Stacie's voice. I would not allow him to silence her. I had never felt such raw emotions toward another human being.

## Chapter 19
# POMC Chapter

*"Very truly I tell you, you will weep and mourn while the world rejoices. You will grieve, but your grief will turn to joy."*
John 16:20 (ESV)

While bouncing from one grief support group to another, I learned about an organization called Parents of Murdered Children. After researching the organization, I learned they held annual conferences each year around the United States. The next conference would be held in August in Oklahoma City, Oklahoma. The cost of the registration fee plus travel was out of our budget. I prayed the Lord would help us find a way. I had recently shared the information with the Prince William County Victim Witness Director Patty Allue. Patty and her staff were so helpful. A few weeks later Patty called and said the Kiwanis Club members donated the funds to cover our air fare and registration fees to attend the 13th Annual POMC National Conference in Oklahoma City. Kristie and I were very excited.

My mom registered and drove from Texas. We met some extraordinary people and made lots of new friends at the conference. For the first time in months, I no longer felt we were walking our journey alone.

We were the youngest survivors, meaning our tragedy was the most recent. It was very healing to be among other parents who were walking a similar journey of grief.

Although each person was at different stages in his/her journey, he/she understood and met us right where we were. During the conference, we met another mother and daughter, Betty and Stephanie, from Virginia. Betty's granddaughters, ages two and three, were brutally murdered by their estranged father. After shooting his daughters in the head, he turned the gun on himself. Betty found support from POMC. Eight years later, Betty started the POMC Shenandoah Valley Chapter and served as chapter leader for many years.

We formed friendships during the conference that we were very grateful for. After being thrown into a realm of horrific suffering, loss, and darkness, we were still desperately trying to learn how to keep from drowning in sorrow. We were still in shock and couldn't find solid ground. Those friendships became life preservers, offering healing, compassion, and a shoulder to cry on from a common bond of pain and grief that we could never have forged alone.

During the conference in Oklahoma City, Kristie and I received an invitation from Betty to attend the Shenandoah Valley Chapter meeting. We promised to attend. After returning home to Virginia, several weeks went by, and Kristie and I finally made the one hour drive to Shenandoah Valley to attend Betty's meeting. I left the conference with a desire to do something positive to help other parents of murdered children but wasn't sure where to start.

We arrived at the church, and everyone was seated in a circle. Every person there had a similar story to share. For two hours we listened to the gruesome details of their children's horrific murders. A woman by the name of Evelyn Guiliani was seated next to Kristie. After I shared our story,

Evelyn introduced herself to us. She shared the story of her daughter's murder. Evelyn was an ER nurse at Inova Fairfax Hospital and was on duty the evening Kristie was brought in by Air-Care on that fateful night.

She described the scene. The twenty-two member trauma team emergency staff was on standby for a fourteen-year-old female with multiple stab wounds who was suffering severe shock due to substantial blood loss and a compromised airway. Kristie was rushed into surgery upon her arrival. When a child arrives in the ER, the staff takes it very hard. They have kids of their own, and it hits a raw nerve. The comments floating around the surgical room were notorious for the circumstances.

After more than four hours of surgery, Dr. Futterman was advised that the parents had arrived at the hospital. He left Kristie in the hands of Dr. Dwyer and Dr. Shabahang. Upon his return to the surgical room, Dr. Futterman was appalled as he stated the mother had no idea what had happened to her daughter after being detained by the police department for more than two hours. He was clearly upset with the lack of compassion the family was shown. It was not his place to describe in detail what this mother's daughter had endured during the attack. She should have been given that information long before she ever arrived here. How does a lack of communication occur when such dire circumstances have occurred? "It's absurd," he said.

## Chapter 20
# Preparing for Trial

*"The truly righteous man attains life but he who pursues evil goes to his death."*
Proverbs 11:19 (ESV)

Our justice system lacks compassion and empathy in relation to victims, survivors, and their families. Their priority is to the criminal. We often joke that is why it's called criminal justice. Powell's trial would be no laughing matter. We wanted justice, but to what extent would we go to get it?

I was excited, anxious, fearful, still in shock, and trying desperately to be brave for Kristie's sake. We were informed the trial would soon be scheduled. In the meantime, the CA's office wanted to meet with us to prepare Kristie for her testimony. She was terrified of testifying in front of him. We fought the best we could to make sure she wouldn't have to face him but to no avail.

One evening, Bobby and I were in my office going over some bills, and Kristie came in. I could tell something was on her mind. My heart broke every time Kristie would ask, "Why do I have to do this?" I tried to express to her that I knew how hard this was going to be, and if I could take her place, I would, but I couldn't. She was the only one who could do this, and she would be the one to put him away.

If he received the death penalty, and chances were very

good, he would be executed. It didn't give her much peace. She still had to face him in court and tell the world what he had done to her and her sister. The nightmares started all over again.

As Kristie turned to leave the room, a framed photo sitting behind other photos on the top of a bookshelf suddenly leaped over the photos in front of it and onto the floor. We all three looked from the picture frame to each other in utter astonishment. We left the room and closed the door.

A few days later we were called to Mr. Ebert's office to discuss Kristie's testimony. She walked him through the events of January 29, 1999. Kristie gave him the details from the beginning. This was the first time I heard her give all the details at once, and it was heart-wrenching.

"I arrived home and placed my key in the lock when suddenly the door opened, and Paul was standing there. I asked where Stacie was. He replied, 'She's in her room.' I waited for him to step aside, and I went into the house. I walked down the hallway to my sister's room, looked in from the doorway, and found Stacie's room in a mess. Her mirror was lying on the floor shattered, the bed was sideways, and her things were scattered around the floor. Stacie was not there. I turned around to walk over to my room and found Paul standing directly behind me. I stepped around him and found my sister lying on my bedroom floor in a pool of blood. Stacie's eyes were open, but she wasn't breathing.

I dropped my book bag and coat and began to cry. 'I need to call my mom!' Paul told me to shut-up and go to the basement. I went because I didn't want to die. I was terrified, knowing he was going to hurt me. 'He told me to take my clothes off, so I did. I pleaded with him not to hurt me, and then he raped me.'

I interrupted Kristie and said, "No, you were strangled then raped!"

Kristie looked at me with a surprised look. She said, "No Mom, he raped me, then strangled me."

I wasn't sure what to say or do. I was rattled by what Kristie stated. I wanted to scream at someone. Why was I given incorrect information? For over a year, Kristie and I had never talked about the rape. I didn't believe she remembered it and didn't feel like we needed to discuss it. We talked about everything else but never the rape. My heart sunk. I felt I had failed my daughter once again.

Kristie mentioned later we didn't talk about it because it was too painful for me. We were trying to protect each other.

Kristie continued. "We heard someone knocking on the back door upstairs. Paul got up, quickly dressed, and grabbed the knife off the dryer. He grabbed my shoes, cut the laces, tied me up, and went upstairs. Just as Paul left the basement, I heard Markey calling my name. I was so scared for him and me. I didn't know what Paul would do to him."

Markey had come into the house, looking for Kristie. "We were supposed to meet outside and play basketball." Paul would later confess to the police he had intended on killing Markey because Powell didn't want any witnesses. Markey, not realizing he narrowly escaped being murdered, figured Kristie had changed her mind, so he closed the door and left.

Kristie managed to get one hand free and tried to scoot across the floor toward the stairwell to hide because she thought he was leaving. When she heard him coming back down the steps, she put her hand back in the shoestring and laid down where she had been.

Paul grabbed her by the shoulders, rolled her onto her stomach, and put something around her neck. He thrust his knee into her back and started choking her until she blacked out.

When she woke up, she heard someone walking around upstairs. Something heavy was lying on top of her, and she couldn't move. She thought Paul was still in the house and could hear him walking around.

Then she heard Bobby's voice, as he came down the stairs. She tried to call out to him, but her voice was very faint. Bobby found her in the basement, nude, tied up, and lying under three bicycles. She was terrified and tried to tell him she wanted to leave the house. She was cold, shaking, and terrified that Powell was coming back. She tried to tell Bobby that they needed to leave.

Bobby asked her where the phone was, and she attempted to look behind her toward the dryer where Paul had laid it. Bobby said, "Don't move. There's blood everywhere, and I don't know how bad you are injured."

Bobby found it and called 9-1-1, but the call was immediately disconnected. The phone was dead. He said he had to leave to find the other phone and that he would be right back. She tried to scream "Nooo!" but could only whisper.

"I have to call 9-1-1; we need help."

He left and came back, and the phone rang; it was 9-1-1. The police finally came and asked if she knew who had done this? She whispered, "Paul Powell."

As we began to prepare for Powell's upcoming trial, the local newspaper reported some interesting facts regarding his stay in the county jail pending his trial date. The Prince William County Sheriff Stoffregen stated, "Powell definitely comes to court with an attitude with a total lack of respect for law enforcement officers and the judicial system, and extra precautions will be taken during the trial."

Paul had threatened to kill jail guards, and at one point, was able to unlock his cell door at the Prince William-Manassas Regional Jail according to jail records. Powell was escorted by more than the usual number of sheriff's deputies as he was transported between the jail and courthouse. "If Powell is cooperative, he won't be restrained," Stoffregen said. "But if he acts inappropriately, deputies have various avenues of restraining any inmate who acts unruly," the sheriff said.

"We are prepared to handle, we think, any situation that might arise in the courtroom," Stoffregen said. "We have access to numerous things that we can do to make sure that he is cooperative with us--that hopefully we don't have to use."

We learned during the trial that Paul not only attempted to break out of his cell, but that he was planning to kill a Hispanic sheriff's deputy because of his race. They found a toothbrush with a sharpened end. Paul later told another inmate that he planned on stabbing the deputy in the neck because Paul wanted to watch the deputy bleed to death.

Because of Paul's attempts to break out of jail, Kristie was even more terrified of him. "I knew I had to testify against Paul at the trial. I was so scared he would find a way to get out and come after me and kill me. Mr. Ebert said they would protect me, but I didn't know if he could really protect me. I wanted this to all be over with. I wanted my sister, Stacie, back. I wanted someone to kill him."

After going over Kristie's testimony for the trial, I advised the CA I wanted to look at the crime scene photos before the trial so that I wasn't caught off guard again.

I was so worried that I could possibly cause a mistrial should I do something wrong. I wanted and needed to be completely prepared for any bombshells they were likely to drop. They adamantly and repeatedly told me no, they could not allow me to view any photos prior to the trial. I refused to accept no for an answer. We had a very heated discussion around this issue. I sternly advised Mr. Ebert and Mr. Willet that I was not leaving until I viewed the photos, and I would do whatever I had to do for *our rights*. I was not going to bow my head and silently sulk away. I inquired of them both what they would do if they were in my situation. They excused themselves to discuss the matter in private. An hour later they returned. I think they'd hoped I would give up and leave but not a chance.

They finally agreed. I was shown photos of Stacie's body lying on Kristie's bedroom floor just as she had been described by Bobby, Kristie, and Detective Leonard. The photos of Stacie were shocking. However, I resiliently composed myself. It made her death final, even though I wasn't ready to accept the fact she was dead.

The other photos that I was shown were of the entire crime scene: Our home. They followed the path the girls took after they both arrived home: Stacie's letter jacket hanging on the back of the dining room chair, her broken watch, and the area in which they found it, her pager, her broken nail, and bedroom. I was shown photos of Kristie after her surgery of her neck, abdomen, and wrists, the stitches clearly visible, while she was in the hospital. Mr.

Willet explained the jury needed to see Paul's attempt to murder her. I got it. I felt it wasn't anything I couldn't handle.

After the trial began, my ability to *"handle it"* almost caused a nervous breakdown. I was not in the least bit prepared for the bombshells the prosecution would drop.

The photos I was shown were in my opinion sugarcoated. I felt betrayed, lied to, and undermined.

## Chapter 21

# Commonwealth of Virginia vs. Paul Warner Powell

The trial began Monday, May 1, 2000, and started with the tedious process of choosing the jury. The jury selection consisted of a pool of about forty potential jurors. Two distinct people stood out to me during the process of the jury selection. One young woman, later to be identified as Mrs. Day, came dressed rather scantily in a crop top, very short skirt, high heels, and a pony tail. I hoped she would not be selected. I was appalled she showed up for court dressed like that.

The other potential juror was an older African American man, whose name I was never able to obtain. When questioned through the jury selection process, he told the court his father had been murdered years prior. I was very excited about this man and prayed he would be selected for the jury panel. Both were chosen as jurors. Mrs. Day was appointed the jury forewoman. She was a legal secretary for a law firm in Washington, D.C. This would prove to be a big mistake.

On Tuesday, May 2, 2000, Bobby was called as the State's first witness. He testified he had returned home from work shortly after 4:00 p.m., finding the mail had not been checked, and the back door was unlocked. This was not normal. The cordless phone wasn't in the kitchen; however, the missing phone was typical, as the girls would leave it in their bedrooms periodically. Bobby always called me as soon as he got home. He never made the call to me that day.

He headed for Stacie's room to look for the phone and found the same disarray Kristie had found. As he turned to check Kristie's room, he found Stacie. He shook her trying to revive her and realized she wasn't breathing. He yelled, "S***," as he dashed down the stairs. Hearing a faint noise that sounded like his name being called, he stopped halfway down and listened. He heard it again and ran into the basement where he found Kristie, lying on the floor, under a pile of bicycles, her feet bound, neck slit, and two wounds to her stomach.

The 9-1-1 call was played. It was very emotional as I had not heard the 9-1-1 call until that day. As Bobby frantically tried to ask for help, the dispatcher was trying to understand what the emergency was. He answered her questions and asked for help, and Kristie was moaning in the back ground.

Bobby was pleading with her to send help. Police and rescue had been dispatched, but to Bobby and Kristie it was an eternity. It was agonizing sitting there listening to the call, which seemed to go on forever. The jurors were crying as were most everyone in the courtroom. It was extremely painful emotionally.

I wasn't sure I could sit through much more of Bobby's testimony and uncertain I could make it through Kristie's. By the grace of God, He gave me the strength.

Kristie was called as the next witness. Mr. Ebert had a plan. Kristie did not want to have to look at Paul Powell and was adamant she was not going to. Mr. Ebert worked it out, and when she was called as the next witness, Mr. Ebert met her at the courtroom doors, put Kristie on his left side with his arm around her shoulders, and protected her. He walked her around in front of the jurors, in front of the judge's bench, and over to the witness stand.

In Virginia, the witness stand sits but a few feet in front of the defense table. The reasoning, we were told, is the defendant has the right to face his accuser. What rights did Kristie have? We found out very few. We asked to have Kristie's testimony taped or given by closed circuit TV, but the judge would not allow it. It turned out Powell didn't have the guts to look up at anybody during the entire trial except the judge, whom he was required to face.

Once Kristie was seated in the witness stand, Mr. Ebert walked back over to the farthest corner in front of the jurors, and at the end of the judge's bench, he held up an 8"x10" photo and asked Kristie to identify the person in it. She said it was Paul Powell, the defendant.

Then she stared directly at the jurors. Kristie told them what happened during the attack. Jurors wiped their eyes as Kristie began to cry on the witness stand, recounting Powell's statement to her upon finding her sister's motionless body. "He told me to go downstairs" she said. "I went because I didn't want to die."

Mr. Ebert asked Kristie to show jurors the scars that still covered her neck. She stated she was still suffering from pain in her stomach, and part of her throat and neck were numb.

Several more witnesses were called including me. I testified that Stacie had just received her paycheck from her part-time job a few days prior to her attack. The money, $37, was not found. The prosecuting attorneys were also trying to prove robbery.

Powell had been living with a friend, Brian, in

Spotsylvania County. Brian was a knife collector and testified that he routinely let Powell carry two of his knives. He also testified that Powell had made derogatory comments about racial minorities and "claimed to be" a white supremacist. On January 29, 1999, Brian woke up to find that Powell had left, and his 9mm pistol and a car owned by another roommate were gone.

Detective Leonard testified that after Paul attacked my daughters, he went upstairs, made himself a glass of iced tea, called for a cab to pick him up, and smoked a cigarette. He then hung out with his friend, Kevin, who testified. When Kevin asked Powell about a bruise on his face, Powell commented he had gotten into a fight with some b****. Kevin testified that they drove to Washington, D.C., and Powell bought drugs; then they went to Kevin's girlfriend's house in Manassas, a few short miles from our house. Kevin testified that they watched the news, and the story of the girls' attack came on. Kevin joked "Why did you do that, Paul?" He had no idea Powell was actually involved.

Police were at Powell's Mother's house when the owner of the car showed up to see if Powell was there. They told police of the missing car and gun. One young lady said she was familiar with where Powell sometimes hung out, but she didn't know the exact address. An officer agreed to drive her through a townhouse complex that evening. It was dark outside, and she happened to see him through an upstairs bedroom window. He was packing to leave town.

The officer called in the location. The S.W.A.T. Team was called out. While they waited Paul out, a young man attempted to make a pizza delivery to Kevin's girlfriend's house. The police paid for the pizza and consumed it. A short while later, Kevin came out on the porch to smoke a cigarette. The S.W.A.T. Team apprehended him and questioned him. They learned there were a young woman and her two young daughters in the house with Powell. They waited a while longer.

They guessed Powell would wonder what happened to Kevin; he eventually stepped out on the porch. As he was about to light a smoke, he was apprehended by the S.W.A.T. Team and taken into custody.

A forensic scientist testified that Stacie's blood was found on the sheath of Powell's knife. During these testimonies, Paul showed little reaction, even to the photos of the girls. Paul refused to allow the defense to call his parents to testify on his behalf and told his attorneys not give any closing arguments. The capital murder trial of Paul Warner Powell lasted more than a week.

Jurors deliberated for days before the verdict was finally read: The jury found Paul Warner Powell guilty of capital murder in the murder of Stacie. He was found guilty for the charges against Kristie and sentenced to three consecutive life sentences for her abduction, rape, and attempted murder.

The jurors then had to decide if Powell should be given life in prison or the death penalty. On the final day of the trial and four and half more hours of deliberation, the jury came back with his sentence. The verdict: Powell received the death penalty. He was given what he asked for. Our family was greatly relieved.

We were scheduled to return in August 2000, and Judge Whisenant, Jr. would sentence Powell to death, but the sentencing would be postponed until October 2000. In October, I was prepared to read my impact statement. I was going to let Paul know exactly what I thought and how I felt about him as a human being.

After we arrived at the court house, I was pulled aside by Mr. Ebert. He said, "Lorraine, I don't think you're going to want to read your impact statement." I almost screamed at him. How could he possibly for one second *think* I wouldn't want to read my impact statement? Had he lost his mind? I know the trial was horrific, but this man has put more murders on death row than any other prosecutor. What could he possibly be thinking? He obviously doesn't know me very well.

I gathered my wits and said, "Mr. Ebert, why would you think I would not want to read my impact statement?" I could tell it was difficult for him to express what it was he needed to say, but the look on his face brought fear to my heart.

Without looking at me, which was very unlike him, he said, "There has been a turn of events." I couldn't begin to imagine what could be so terrible that he would even speak those words. Then he said, "The jury foreman has fallen in love with Powell."

I almost swallowed my tongue. My heart dropped to my feet, and I felt my pulse racing. My legs became weak. I began to shake all over. My mind was racing. His words cut through me like a double-edged sword. Mr. Ebert pulled a chair under me and helped me to sit down. I couldn't begin to wrap my mind around the words he had just spoken, much less begin to comprehend how this *woman* could possibly have fallen in love with Paul Powell!

It took me a few minutes to compose myself. I felt a surge of rage that consumed me. I wanted to find this woman. How could she? What would possess her...? Mr. Ebert began to reveal the facts of the past six months.

Chapter 22
# The Witch Testifies

*"Do not turn to mediums or seek out spirits, for you will be defiled by them. I am the Lord your God."*
Leviticus 19:31 (ESV)

We eagerly waited for the judge's decision on the sentencing phase of Powell's conviction. Emotions were running rampant as we agonizingly awaited Mrs. Day taking the witness stand to testify on Powell's behalf. I was appalled that Paul's court-appointed defense attorneys, Morrissette and Fahy, would stoop this low.

Mrs. Day took the witness stand before the judge formally imposed the death sentence and swore to God that she loved this rapist and murderer and that this man she had condemned really didn't deserve to die. "It's twisted, I know," said Day.

When Kristie took the witness stand, Day stated she cried silent tears. "I was so hurt by what had been done to her. The whole time I was giving Paul the meanest look I could possibly give. . . . I thought at the point that he should die."

Day testified for more than an hour that she misunderstood the sentencing instructions and said she felt the law required her to sentence Paul to death. Later she stated she had read in the instructions that Paul could have been sentenced to death or life without parole.

I recall the jury sending notes back to Judge Whisenant during the jury's deliberations, asking questions regarding the instructions. The court would be called back into session and the questions read.

This was excruciating because each time we were called back into the courtroom, we thought the jury had reached a verdict, only to learn it was yet another question from the jury.

After the third question, it was very apparent Judge Whisenant was becoming agitated with the questions and advised the jury they were given clear instructions, and they needed to read them. He would not allow any more questions from the jury.

Mr. Ebert told the court that after the jury was dismissed from the trial, Mrs. Day walked straight to the jail and requested to see Powell and wanted to give him money for toiletries. Powell was still sitting in the courtroom. That was when things began to unfold.

She testified that after the verdicts were read and the jury was dismissed, she suddenly began feeling guilty for asking for the death sentence. During the sentencing phase of his trial when Powell told his attorneys not to present any evidence on his behalf, Mrs. Day said that bothered her; she thought the attorneys just hadn't done their job.

In his defense, she stated, "I'm thinking of him not in terms of being a murderer but that this is a real person who has tastes and ideas and could have made a life for himself. He did something inhumane and crossed the line, but you can like things about him that aren't murderous—he has redeeming qualities. And even though I like him now, I will never condone anything he's done. And I do think he should pay for it."

Mr. Ebert presented copies of letters between Mrs. Day and Powell she wrote him at the Prince William-Manassas Regional Jail. Day wrote Powell, asking if he would talk to her. Powell wrote back quickly that read in part, "I don't have any friends anymore because of what I've done, so it would be nice to have someone to write and talk to."

Shortly, thereafter, more than a dozen letters were exchanged between Day and Powell in a three-month span. In one letter dated July 5, Powell wrote to Mrs. Day that began, "Hey beautiful. I think you are right when you say we are soul mates. I can't believe someone as beautiful as you and as smart as you has fallen in love with someone like me."

Powell added Day to his call list, and then the daily calls began. Day and Powell talked every day for two hours. At first it was "getting to know you" chit chat with questions, such as what were his days like in jail? What kind of music did she like? Day said she soon began to realize the commonalities they shared. He made her laugh, sometimes hysterically. "It showed me he was alive, and he is a person. It made him seem real. And all I wanted and still want is to give him some hope."

In another letter, he said, "I love you, and I'm not ashamed to say it. You mean everything to me. I don't know what I would do without you."

At his request, Day sent him $70 and talked to him about the possibility of visiting him in prison. The relationship from Powell's point of view had reached a new level, and he immediately placed her on his visitation and call list.

Mr. Ebert questioned Mrs. Day about her religion and how she converted Powell. Mrs. Day practiced Wicca, a form of witchcraft. I almost yelled out but caught myself. Who would take the stand and testify to such crap?

She sent him anti-death penalty articles she printed off the Internet to give him hope that he may not have to die. She told Powell she would try to help him avoid the death penalty.

Mrs. Day testified that she and Powell last spoke on Wednesday, August 9, 2000, for more than an hour on the phone and that she planned to continue her relationship with Powell but did not plan physical contact. "It's a very unique situation," she told Ebert during her testimony.

"It sure is," Ebert replied.

I couldn't bring myself to look at Powell, and I put my head in my hands, still trying to digest this -- whatever it was. The courtroom was as astounded as we were. Folks began murmuring, shifting in their seats, and glancing at each other in utter disgust.

When I was later interviewed, I was still shocked, and all I could say was, "I still cannot believe that anybody could love an animal that does something like this. Her testimony was appalling to me."

I wanted remorse, and this is what we got instead. He sat there looking completely blank. I asked myself if I were living in a soap opera. Things like this don't happen in real life.

The defense asked Judge Whisenant to discard the jury verdict and give Powell life in prison and stated Powell was diagnosed with psychological problems at a young age and was abused by his father.

But Mr. Ebert argued Powell had been given many chances by the juvenile justice system. He reminded the judge that Powell said he had plans to kill the girls' mother and step-father and noted that he had shown no remorse. Mr. Ebert read from Kristie's victim impact statement.

"I will never see my sister again, see her graduate from high school, get married, or have children." Kristie wrote.

Mr. Ebert said after the hearing, "This case is an extremely vile case. The death penalty is not for everybody. It's reserved for the vile of the vile."

In Mr. Ebert's cross examination of Mrs. Day's testimony in Powell's defense, he made her look like a complete fool. Mr. Ebert stated to the press when interviewed, "Her testimony and relationship with Powell made her a biased witness. It's pretty clear that I think she fell in love with him, and he definitely fell in love with her."

Mrs. Day's signature rests on the jury's conviction that will ultimately send him to death row:

COMMONWEALTH OF VIRGINIA
CRIMINAL NO. 45693
vs.
PAUL WARNER POWELL

We, the jury, on the issue joined, having found the defendant guilty of Capitol Murder in the Commission of Rape and having unanimously of wantonly vile, horrible or inhuman in that it involved torture, depravity of mind, or aggravated battery to the victim beyond the minimum to accomplish the act of death and having considered the evidence in mitigation of the offense, unanimously fix his punishment at death.

J. Day
Foreman

Mrs. Day stated later that worse than watching Kristie testify and leave the courtroom in disgust and hearing criticism from Kristie's Mother for loving the "animal" who destroyed her family and worse than the embarrassment of testifying was the attention she got in local newspapers the next day. Really?

The media couldn't wait to talk to Kristie and me. The only question they really wanted to know was, "Are you still planning to attend his execution?" Really!

## Chapter 23
# Grief

*"My eyes have grown dim with grief; my whole frame is but a shadow."*
Job 17:7 (ESV)

Grief is defined as "deep mental anguish, as that arising from bereavement," as defined by *Webster's Dictionary.*

Compounded by the fact my daughters were brutally attacked, Stacie was dead, and Kristie's life forever scarred by the heinous acts of Paul Powell and having heard Mrs. Day's testimony added to my daily struggles to cope. Before the sentencing, I was able to mask the pain that was heavily taking its toll. It affected my relationship with my daughter, husband, family, and friends.

As Job described his heartache, I related to him wholeheartedly. My entire world had been shattered into a million fragments like the shattered mirror lying on Stacie's bedroom floor. As I stood in the tunnel of darkness, consumed by grief and despair, I gazed at the broken glass that reflected my life. Dimly lit by a slither of light, the broken pieces of shard glass represented my brokenness, hopelessness, and heartache. I couldn't comprehend how our lives could ever be pieced back together. How could I continue to go on? How would Kristie and I ever recover from such horrific circumstances?

Grief is a battle of unfamiliar emotions and despairing

feelings of anguish. Turmoil consumes your life, sucking every breath from you, second by second. The very moment the horrific news was spoken, the grief overwhelmed me to the point I couldn't comprehend. I couldn't think straight.

In an attempt to stay sane, I desperately struggled with basic and simple motions of what was familiar. The simplest of tasks that had become second nature to me, like showering, dressing, and putting on makeup, took all the strength I could possibly muster. I went to bed, but sleep was futile. I got up, but I couldn't figure out what to do with myself. I cooked, but no one ate. Everything seemed pointless and redundant. I felt useless and hopeless.

I tried to stay busy, but the house seemed eerie and daunting. Depression was quickly pulling me into total darkness. My mind could not stop envisioning all the horrific accounts at the trial. Flashes of the photos of Stacie's body in the morgue went through my mind constantly, as well as Kristie being on the witness stand and terrified. And all I was allowed to do was sit quietly, listen, and wait.

I relived those horrific events in my mind moment by moment, day after day. I could not concentrate and was barely functioning. I felt like an outcast to my friends, as they purposefully avoided me like the plague. What had I done or said to push them away?

It wasn't me at all. The truth was they had no idea what to say or do around me. They were afraid to mention Stacie's name or talk about Kristie. But I needed them to talk to me, ask me whatever questions they had. I needed to hear them talk about the girls and circumstances. I needed to know I still mattered to them.

The depression was overwhelming! I knew I needed counseling. I couldn't cope with all those horrible thoughts running rampant in my mind. As sleep was not an option, neither was prescription medication. I certainly wasn't going to add to or alter the problem further. I cried for months and tried to pray, but the words seemed completely void. Eventually, I resolved to commit suicide. It seemed the only answer.

I became very sick and spent two entire days in bed. I didn't eat or drink anything. Bobby finally got me up and took me to the doctor. The nurse couldn't find my pulse, and my blood pressure wouldn't register. My lungs were compressed, and I was having difficulty breathing. The doctor came in immediately and began to assess my condition. He ordered x-rays and a battery of tests. I answered his questions as best I could. Bobby finally pulled him aside and shared what we had been through over the past two years. He said he thought I looked familiar. This shed a lot more light on things.

The x-rays showed I had bronchitis, and my pulse and blood pressure readings were due to severe dehydration. The doctor asked if I were being treated for depression. No. I was seeing a counselor but refused to take medication for the symptoms. He said he could give me something to help. I refused his offer repeatedly. I just wanted to go home. I was kept at the doctor's office all day. They pumped two bags of fluids into my system to keep me out of the hospital. I was finally released to go home with strict instructions to lie still for six to eight days, as I was also diagnosed with pleurisy and shingles. I was in excruciating pain. The doctor was fairly certain I was suffering from depression.

I spent six days at home on my back trying to heal, but the coughing was the worst. I kept hoping I could cough up my lungs. Maybe the pain would subside.

What I failed to realize was I was suffering spiritual warfare. I believed the lies of the enemy. He was wreaking havoc on my body, torturing my mind and heart.

Bobby was drowning in his own vat of depression. Due to my own grief, I couldn't see how desperately he was struggling. We were like two ships crossing in the night, neither sure what to say or how to express our grief to the other. Desperately afraid of pushing the other one off the edge, we were both teetering on. The ledge was rapidly crumbling beneath our feet and falling in separate directions.

## Chapter 24
# America's Most Wanted

*"Though one may be overpowered, two can defend themselves. A cord of three strands is not quickly broken."*
Ecclesiastes 4:12 (ESV)

Kristie and I were invited to attend the Northern Virginia Victims' Rights Memorial Service hosted by Fairfax Police Department Victim Witness Agency. Our key note speaker was John Walsh of *America's Most Wanted* (AMW). After the ceremony, Kristie and I were standing in line, hoping to talk to Mr. Walsh. We shared a common bond – we were both homicide survivors since his son, Adam, had been murdered. While standing at the back of the long line, a lady approached us, asking if we were Lorraine and Kristie. I replied "Yes," uncertain who was asking. She introduced herself as Cheri Nolan, Mr. Walsh's personal assistant. She asked if we could accompany her to the stage.

I must have had a strange look on my face. She said Mr. Walsh would like to speak to us. Kristie and I looked at each other for a moment, not sure what to say or do. Suddenly and in unison, we both said, "YES!"

Mr. Walsh was familiar with our story and knew Kristie had recently testified as the key witness at Powell's trial. He acknowledged Kristie's bravery and asked if she ever thought about helping others. Not sure what he was asking, she said, "No."

He asked, "Would you consider it?"

She said hesitantly, "Sure." Thinking this was the end of the conversation, she asked if she could get her picture taken with him.

He asked, "Have you considered my request?"

"No," she replied. Smiling, he agreed to the photos.

As it turned out, he was working on a case involving a young girl of nine, who was brutally attacked December 1999 in Del Rio, Texas, and she was the only survivor. The victim was identified as nine-year-old Krystal. Mr. Walsh briefly shared Krystal's story, and we were amazed at the similarity of our stories.

Mr. Walsh felt Kristie and Krystal should meet. Since Kristie had recently testified against Powell, he felt she could help Krystal prepare for her testimony against her offender. We knew we needed to help this family.

In August 2002, the meeting was arranged. I was uncomfortable bringing the media into our home, so we arranged to meet in Bull Run Park. Kristie and I arrived early to meet the camera team. As we anxiously awaited their arrival, the suspense was mounting. Suddenly, a distance away, winding along the road, slowly making its way toward us, we spotted a sleek black car coming through the trees. The AMW cameras were ready to capture the girls' first meeting. As the car came to a stop, the door slowly opened. We had not seen or spoken to this family before this meeting. Everything was arranged through AMW. The door opened and out stepped this tiny, slender, blond-haired, blue-eyed, little girl, wearing glasses and the cutest smile. Kristie was about fifty yards in front of me. I was out of camera range, so they could get the perfect shot of the girls' meeting. As soon as Krystal stepped out of the car, Kristie and I both did a double take. Kristie looked back at me, and our mouths were hanging open, just staring. It was the most incredible scene unfolding before us.

Krystal was the spitting image of Stacie at age eleven. We both thought we had seen a ghost. I still cry, and the goose bumps rise up on my arms every time I think about Krystal stepping out of that car and seeing my daughter, Stacie, at age eleven again. It took me back five years to a time when our lives were untouched by the evil of this world.

Her hair, her little glasses, her walk, her expressions, and especially her smile, were the spitting image of Stacie! Everyone who had known Stacie at that age agreed, especially our family members.

We spent the day together with Pam, Krystal, and AMW, filming with the girls getting to know each other. The more we got to know Krystal, the more we learned how much alike she and Stacie really were. During the filming of the show, Krystal became mesmerized by Kristie's ring: A small silver dangle ring with a cross.

There's a story behind that ring I have to share with you. My sister, Theresa, was helping Kristie with her hair the day of Stacie's funeral. Kristie saw Theresa's ring and asked if she could wear it. My sister being my sister, the most unselfish person I know, put it on Kristie's finger. Theresa had no idea how much that ring would come to mean.

After the taping of the show, we parted from their company, having made some extraordinary friends, only to go our separate ways. Pam and Krystal were flying home to Kansas the next day. We agreed to stay in touch.

We learned they had a layover in Dallas-Fort Worth (DFW) for a few hours. So I called my mom to tell her about our exciting news of meeting Pam and Krystal. I asked my mom if she would do me a favor.

Mom agreed to our plan. I told her she would recognize Krystal as soon as Mom saw her. The next day, Pam and Krystal's flight landed at DFW; they had no idea we had devised a plan for my family to meet them at the airport. They had a long layover. As they were heading toward their next gate, Krystal heard her name being called. She looked around, but didn't see anyone she knew. I had given my mom their flight information. She was very skeptical, thinking I was out of my mind. This young girl could not possibly resemble Stacie that much.

My mom and sister, Theresa, finally got Pam and Krystal's attention. They spent over two hours with them, going over family pictures mostly of Stacie. They left convinced the girls were definitely a lot alike, and my mom was convinced I hadn't lost my mind after all.

Pat Llama called to let us know Krystal would be testifying against the perpetrator at the trial in September. Krystal wanted Kristie and me to be there, but we couldn't get away. AMW decided they would be there to film it. The show "America's Littlest Heroes," which was highlighting Krystal's story, would air in November. We were very anxious and excited for Krystal.

Kristie and I decided because we couldn't be there, we would send Krystal our support. I called my sister, Theresa, and she agreed to help us. We invited Pat Llama in on our secret. Pat told the producers of AMW about our plan of support, and they agreed it needed to be filmed. Krystal thought it was just another part of the show. Of course, we wouldn't get to see the surprise until the show aired. And in November, we gathered around the TV, anxiously awaiting the airing of *America's Most Wanted* and our favorite little hero.

The night before Krystal was to testify, they filmed Pam going over Krystal's testimony for the following day, giving her assurance as only a mother could give her daughter. We knew she was in God's hands, and she would do fine. Pat told Krystal she had a surprise for her from a family who was praying for them. Krystal was clueless. Pat handed Krystal a small gift-wrapped box. Krystal looked unsure at the box and then opened it. It was the moment we had been waiting for! She peered in and lying nestled in a small cloth bag was a silver dangle ring with a cross, exactly like the one Kristie, my mom, my sisters, Theresa and Dannene, and I wear. She shouted and immediately showed it to her mom. They both began to cry, as did we! We knew Krystal would testify the next day and put Tommy Lynn Sells away. She did just that.

Krystal took the witness stand with a jagged pink scar across her neck. She bravely testified about the murder of her friend Katy and how Sells slashed her own throat. She looked Sells in the eye as she testified and calmly pointed him out as the perpetrator. Sells was convicted of capital murder and sentenced to death.

Krystal, Katy, and their families will always have a special place in our hearts.

## Chapter 25
# Conviction Overturned?

*"Like apples of gold in settings of silver is a ruling rightly given."* Proverbs 25:11 (ESV)

In April 2001, I received a call from Mr. Ebert. "Lorraine, I'm on my way back from Richmond, Virginia. I had a meeting with the attorney general's office regarding Powell's capital murder conviction. Instantly, I was on high alert. The tone of his voice sounded sad, almost angry. I became very apprehensive and knew when Mr. Ebert called, we likely had a problem regarding Powell's case.

I asked him what was wrong. Mr. Ebert asked me to meet him at his office after work, and we could discuss the matter. I asked him how long until he arrived back at the office? I was too apprehensive to wait until after work to hear the details. Something was wrong, I could feel it. We met a couple of hours later, and Mr. Ebert proceeded to tell me the Virginia Supreme Court had ruled on Powell's sentencing, and it was not good news.

"Now what?" I exclaimed!

He told me that the Virginia Supreme Court ruled against and reversed Powell's capital murder conviction. "No way! Why? How could this happen? I don't understand. How could this happen? It was a solid case. What did we miss?"

Mr. Ebert explained that based on their ruling, they

could not find enough evidence to uphold his conviction for the charges of Stacie's murder and the charges of attempted rape. In view of the Virginia Supreme Court, to uphold a conviction of capital murder, there has to be a felony in the commission of a murder. The felony in Paul's case was "rape." Stacie was murdered, but she was not raped. Kristie was raped, but she was not murdered, and they were viewing this as two separate cases.

I argued, "It was not two separate cases. Powell didn't leave the house after murdering Stacie. He waited over two hours and attacked Kristie. He never left the house during that period. He waited!"

Mr. Ebert advised the ruling was made, and Powell would get another trial. Kristie and Bobby would have to testify again. There was nothing we could do at this point. He would keep us posted. I was devastated. I had to break this devastating news to Kristie.

I asked Mr. Ebert what would be the maximum punishment we could get in a new trial? He said, "First degree, which would be life in prison."

Kristie was going to be crushed. She had done everything the courts asked her to. She'd stood before judge, jury, and the defendant, with the eyes of the media all over her. She'd testified to the world, through tears and fears, what Paul had done to her. The Commonwealth built a case based on solid evidence of what he had done to Stacie, the brutality and horror of his crime. And now the Virginia Supreme Court ruled there's not enough evidence to uphold his capital murder conviction?

Where was the justice for Stacie and Kristie? What was wrong with our justice system? I didn't understand. I prayed that God would help us through this nightmare once again.

I sat Kristie down in an attempt to explain to her what had happened.

She was furious. We cried together, and we clung to each other, trying to make sense of our justice system. I tried to explain that even if the best we got was first degree against Powell, he would never get out of prison. I begin to realize how terrified my daughter was at the thought that he could possibly get out of prison and come after her. I tried to reassure her that would not happen. However, I had told her if she testified that one time, she would never have to face him again. I had failed her. She tried to tell me she understood, but I could see she was about to explode.

I called Mr. Ebert and asked if Kristie could come in and talk to him. He stayed late that night, so we could meet with him and Kristie could drill him with questions. After we left his office, I could see she was much more at ease, although she felt he, too, had failed her.

A few days later after praying and asking the Lord to give Kristie peace about this overturned conviction, the Lord put it on my heart to talk to Kristie more in depth about the possibility of Powell receiving a life sentence.

I explained to her that a life sentence for an inmate is not an easy ride by any means. "Being on death row," I explained, "means having your own personal cell, where you are locked away from everyone. You have little to no contact with very few people." She didn't seem to be following me. So I tried to explain it in a way she would better understand.

"If he is sentenced to life in prison, he will be put in general population, which means he will be with lots of other criminals. Most people don't take lightly to someone who has harmed children. They are going to do such bad things to him that he will wish he was dead and will suffer greatly."

I didn't get the sense she understood. I told her if you need to talk about it, I'm always here to talk anytime. Or if you feel you need to talk to Mr. Ebert, he's a phone call away, and it's a short drive to his office.

A few days later, she came to me and said, "Mom, I was talking to some of my friends about Paul getting life in prison, and I think I'm okay with that." I looked at her for a minute, not sure what to think. And then she said, "My friends told me what they do to people like Paul who hurt kids."

I got it. She got it! I laughed, and hugged her. I wasn't prepared for that one, but the Lord took care of it His way. I could only imagine the details they gave Kristie, but after all she had been through, she needed to know she was safe.

We met with Mr. Ebert periodically over the next few months. He would call and ask how we were doing and to check on us. I greatly appreciated knowing we were on his and many other's hearts. We were still receiving cards and letters from people praying for us.

## Chapter 26
# Marriage to Divorce

*"A man's enemies will be the members of his own household...."*
Matthew 10:36 (ESV)

Bobby and I met while working together and several months later began dating. Marriage was the farthest thing from my mind. Bobby had never married and had no children. He worked a full and a part-time job. Bobby proposed after two years of dating, but I wasn't interested. My parents' marriage ended in divorce after seventeen years, and my first marriage had ended after eleven years. My parent's marriage ended because of my dad's infidelity. My first marriage ended due to the same reason. Trust was a huge issue for me. However, after dating for four years, I was beginning to consider his proposal.

In 1992, while living in Arkansas and married to my first husband, the girls' dad, I had received a call that my dad, who was living in Virginia, was having emergency surgery. He had suffered an aortic aneurysm and was essentially bleeding to death. My relationship with my dad was almost non-existent, which had stemmed from his leaving mom and us in 1978 due to an extramarital affair on his part. I had a lot of resentment toward my dad, but my sister and I flew to Virginia, and although I was worried about him, I kept my true feelings hidden, only showing him my anger and resentment. When we arrived at the hospital, we were told visiting hours were over, and we would have to come back the following morning. We pleaded with the nurses, advising we had flown all the way from Texas, arriving as soon as we could. We told them he had no family here, and we needed to see him. Dad was in ICU and was heavily sedated with numerous medications. My father struggled with a sensitivity to medication and had many allergic reactions. We had almost lost him twice during the surgery.

The nurse agreed to allow us a quick visit. I wish I had never entered his room. He was completely out of his mind. He was so doped up on medication that he was restrained to the bed. As soon as we walked in, he became quite savage. He was not the dad I had known. To witness him in this state was devastating. He cursed us violently for several minutes, using words I didn't know existed. I was mortified and ran from the room in tears and utter disbelief that this was my dad. It would be two to three days before I would return.

My sister was adamant that we needed to see him. I was not. I refused to go back but finally we did, and he was a completely different person. They discovered the morphine had made him delirious. If they had asked me, I would have told them to commit him to the psychiatric ward and keep him there for the rest of his life. At the time, I had no idea of the relationship with my dad would have such a detrimental effect that would surface after the girls' attack. The following week, Theresa returned home. He was finally moved to a private room.

During the time I spent alone with Dad, I witnessed a radical change from the lunatic I witnessed the first night. Since his admittance was an emergency, and the hospital had never treated him, they had no medical records on file. Dad had no family physician or family in Virginia to inform them of his medical status.

Our family had no information as to his medical condition due to the lack of contact from him. It had been ten years since I had seen my dad. Since becoming a Mom and him a Grandfather, I had come to resent him for never pursuing a relationship with his daughters and grand-daughters. It had been several years since we had spoken to each other, especially face to face. I still harbored a lot of resentment toward him for leaving us and for severing our relationships.

During the week, it was just the two of us, and we had long heart-to-heart talks. I had a captive audience, and I needed answers. For the first time ever he opened up to me, and we shared our cherished memories. Dad talked about his near-death experience during the surgery, which was not his first. He had shared with us kids many times of his near-drowning experience when he was a small child. He admitted he was scared, and he didn't think he would survive the surgery. That was why he had the hospital contact us minutes before he was taken into surgery.

He shared with me that at age thirty-five, he had suffered a midlife crisis, which ultimately ended our parents' marriage. He admitted he had had an extramarital affair with a woman at work and decided to leave Mom, a mistake he would regret the rest of his life. When he realized his mistake, he asked Mom to take him back; she refused, citing she could never trust him again. She asked for a divorce, which he granted her.

My parents were not religious people and did not attend church. They were married for seventeen years and dad threw it all away. He eventually remarried another woman, which ended in divorce. Dad was a very angry person and was known to self-destruct. He had a huge temper. But the man sitting before me was not the man I had known several years ago. He was frail, had lost a lot of weight, and looked older than his fifty-two years.

We decided to work together at rebuilding our relationship. I hoped I would finally have that father-daughter relationship I had tried so desperately to have as a child. The day before I returned home, he invited our family to come visit him in Virginia. He talked about all the places he wanted to show us. He was a freelance photographer and talked extensively about the four seasons and the extravagant colors of fall, the Blue Ridge Mountains, the Chesapeake Bay, and the beautiful beaches. In the short two weeks I got to spend there, I had never seen a more beautiful state. There was so much to look forward to.

Time and life got in the way of our plans, and, of course, we thought we had many more tomorrows left. Two years later, we received another call from Fairfax Hospital in Fairfax, Virginia, advising us dad had yet another aortic aneurysm. We would later learn it was his fourth. He wanted his three daughters to know he loved us very much. My dad died during surgery. He had never told us about the previous two that by the grace of God he had survived.

My marriage to the girls' Dad was in turmoil. My husband of eleven years was having an extramarital affair with his best friend's wife, my best friend. He came home late one night, and I asked him where he had been. He wouldn't admit what I already knew. He had been drinking, and I suspected drugs as well. I threatened to leave him, and he grabbed me by the arms and pushed me up against the wall and told me I had better think twice about it.

He had removed something from the car so it wouldn't run. I couldn't leave, and he forced me to sleep with him. I was terrified he would hurt me if I moved, so I lay awake beside him all night. As soon as he left for work, I called his brother and asked him what was wrong with the car? He said the coil had been removed. I found it under the couch, and his brother put it back on for me. The girls were with my mom in Texas for the summer.

I wasted no time in packing my clothes. I left quickly. This was completely out of character for him. We had had our arguments, but this was over the top. I told him years before if he ever laid a hand on me or the girls, he would never do it again.

After a month of being separated, we agreed to attempt to reconcile our marriage. The same day I moved back home, I received the call that my dad died during surgery.

Dad's death took a huge toll on me. Once again shattered dreams was all I had. My sisters and I traveled back to Virginia to bring Dad's body home to Texas. The second child of four siblings, he was survived by his mom and elder brother.

Fairfax Hospital would play another very important role in our lives nine years later. His granddaughter, Kristie, would also arrive, fighting for her life.

Dad's death left a huge void in my life. After my marriage failed a second time, I left, taking my shattered dreams and a few personal belongings and moved to Virginia to start over. I knew two people, friends of Dad's, and they graciously took me in until I could find a place to live. I was able to transfer with the company I worked for. Eventually, the girls and I made a new life together. Never could I have imagined where our lives would take us.

Bobby and I married in August 1999, and shortly thereafter, I watched my new husband drown his grief in alcohol. He began to withdraw from everyone, including me and Kristie. Our home became his refuge, but it was anything but safe. His drinking became excessive, and the repercussions of the girls' attack created outrages and outbursts between us, blaming each other for our problems and things we couldn't control. Hatred began to unfold. I was desperately searching for support in any and every support group I could find, but Bobby found solace only in alcohol and refused to consider counseling.

Less than a year later, Bobby and I separated. Our relationship was a subject of self-destruction, and we allowed the grief to destroy all of us. By December of 2001, we were divorced.

Chapter 27
# Guest Speaker?

*"In my distress I called to the LORD; I called out to my*
*God. From his temple he heard my voice; my cry came to his*
*ears."*
2 Samuel 22:7 (ESV)

Powell's case was of great interest mostly because of
the brutality of his actions, as well as due to the ongoing
issues he was creating. We, the family, were trying
desperately to find a way to cope with all the attention,
while trying to focus on healing. We strived to bring forth
positive aspects and changes, especially since the police
department didn't know how to handle our family. It was
not a slam to law enforcement agencies, but we quickly
realized certain aspects within the agencies needed
restructuring.

Detective Leonard recognized these issues as well, and
less than three weeks after the girl's attack, he invited me as
a guest speaker to the Police Academy. He advised me to be
brutally honest about the way our family had been treated
during the first seventy-two hours of the tragedy. I went, not
sure if I could do what he was asking. My mom was still in
town and accompanied me.

I was so nervous. I wasn't one to stand before an
audience and give a speech. I was extremely shy. If you
didn't know me, and you were attempting to have a

conversation with me, our eyes would never meet! Unless, of course, I was angry. That day I was angry. I soon realized I had found a way to vent my frustrations, and since the case was still fresh on the officers' minds, and since they knew the mistakes they had made specifically with our family, I could speak candidly, as well as honestly as to how we were treated.

My mom had the opportunity to share her grievances as well, regarding attempts in contacting the hospital and the agony of being out of state. Again, we didn't have cell phones, so communication was much more limited. We were at the mercy of others, which was not focused on our struggles and issues. We depended on them for information, and that information was lacking.

Mom shared the grueling hours of waiting and contacting the hospital, only to be told they had no patient by the name of Kristie. She had no idea we were being detained. We didn't know the issues she was having. She didn't have the phone number of the neighbor's house. I never thought to give it to her. I thought we would be leaving for the hospital shortly after having spoken to her.

The class actually thanked us for coming and sharing our story. Many relayed it helped them tremendously to know where they had failed us. Detective Leonard began to receive requests from other local law enforcement agencies regarding the Powell case, and he asked me to join him.

Detective Leonard spoke from the law enforcement aspect. I spoke as a survivor. Our efforts were greatly rewarded and were making a difference. Several agencies began to apply these changes within their departments.

Each year at the College of William and Mary in Williamsburg, Virginia, Detective Leonard is joined by other instructors for the Murder One class, which is sponsored by the Commonwealth Attorney's Services Council. Detectives are paired with prosecutors in the same jurisdictions. A networking partnership helps facilitate an atmosphere as a way to help them understand each other's role in the justice system.

Many courses are taught, which are relevant to each field. Guest speakers are used to highlight a particular subject or how to deal with the families of homicide victims.

Kristie and I have been invited several times to share our story, frustrations, and issues. One thing I learned very early in law enforcement and through the process of the criminal justice system, was to look beyond the obvious. I enrolled in the Citizens Police Academy and specific classes open to the public to learn more about the operation of our police department.

I learned a great deal. I had many opportunities to share and suggest specific changes. Folks began to recognize me, which also led to many additional invitations to speak, which has taken us all over the United States. There have been times due to specific cases and court dates when Detective Leonard was not able to accompany me. The impact of the presentation lacked greatly. He has since retired, only physically, and is still very active and involved as an instructor and consultant.

All law enforcement agencies are to be commended on the work they do. They have a very difficult job. To protect and serve is not to be taken lightly by the communities they serve. They are very dedicated, experienced, and an elite group of men and women. Thank you for your dedication and service. May God bless you and protect you.

Chapter 28
# Confession

*"In the sight of God, who gives life to everything, and of Christ Jesus, who while testifying before Pontius Pilate made the good confession, I charge you."*
1 Timothy 6:13 (ESV)

In October of 2001, I received a call from Mr. Ebert. "Lorraine, we need to talk. Come to my office after work." This was becoming commonplace with us. I knew when he started his greeting that way, we had a problem again. I told him I would meet him at his office.

I anxiously arrived that evening, anticipating another let down. After being seated in his office, he said he had something he thought I might like to read.

"You can judge for yourself what to make of it." I was not prepared for what I was about to read, but at this point, I didn't think anything else could shock me regarding Paul Powell.

Mr. Ebert handed me a very lengthy, hand-written, four- page letter on legal sized paper. I glanced down at the hand writing and recognized it right away. It was from Paul Powell and addressed to Mr. Ebert. I was curious why he wanted me to read a letter addressed to him. I glanced up with a questioning look on my face. He assured me it was okay to read his letter.

As I begin to read, Mr. Ebert asked me if I would prefer

to be alone. I had gotten as far as the second paragraph and realized why he was asking. I shook my head no, as tears began streaming down my face.

The letter from Powell was taunting Mr. Ebert, and it was just as brutal as his attack on Stacie and Kristie.

*Powell's letter to Mr. Ebert dated October 21, 2001: (Disclaimer: This letter is the actual letter copied from Powell's own handwriting. These are his exact words and misspellings are his. The expletives have been noted as such.)*

Mr. Ebert,

Since I have already been indicted on first degree murder and the VA supreme court says that I can't be charged with capital murder again, I figured I would tell you the rest of what happened on Jan. 29, 1999 to show you how stupid all of y'all (explicit) are. Y'all should have known there was more to the story, than what I told by what I said.

You had it in writing that I planned to kill the whole family. Since I planned to kill the whole family, why would I have fought with Stacie before killing her? She had no idea I was planning to kill everybody, and talked and carried on like usual so I could've stabbed her at any time because she was unsuspecting. I had other plans for her before she died.

When I got to the house, Stacie was on the phone, so I went inside and laid on the couch. She went to her room and got her clothes and went downstairs to do her laundry. When she went downstairs, I got up and shut and locked the back door and went downstairs. We talked while she put her clothes in the wash. We continued talking when she had everything in the wash and I reached over and touched her (explicit) and asked if she wanted to (explicit)? She said no because she had a boyfriend. I started arguing with her because she had never turned anyone down because of having a boyfriend. We started walking upstairs, arguing the whole time. When we got upstairs we went to her room and she turned the radio off.

After she turned the radio off I pushed her onto her bed and grabbed both her wrists and pinned her hands down by her head and sat on top of her. I told her all I wanted to do was (explicit) her and then I would leave and that we could do it the easy way or the hard way. She said she would (explicit) me, so I got up. She started fighting with me and clawed my face. We wrestled around a little and then I slammed her to the floor. When she hit the floor I sat on top of her and pinned her hands down again. She said she would (explicit) me and I told her that if she started fighting with me again I would kill her.

When I got up she stood up and kept asking me why I was doing this and all I kept saying was take your clothes off. Finally she undid her pants and pulled them down to her ankles. She was getting ready to take them the rest of the way off and the phone rang. When she heard the phone she pulled her pants back up and said she had to answer the phone. I pushed her back and said no. She said she wouldn't say anything about me being there and I told her no and to take her clothes off. She tried to get out of the room again and I pushed her back and pulled out my knife. I guess she thought I was trying to scare her and that I wouldn't really stab her because she tried to leave again. When she got to me and tried to squeeze between me and the door jamb I stabbed her.

When I stabbed her she fell back against the door jam and just looked at me with a shocked look on her face. When I pulled the knife out she stumbled a couple of steps and fell into her sister's room. I walked over and looked at her. I saw that she was still breathing so I stepped over her body and into the bedroom. Then I put my foot on her throat so she couldn't breathe. Then I stepped down and started stomping on her throat. Then I stepped back onto her throat and moved up and down putting more pressure to make it harder to breathe. When I didn't see her breathing anymore I left the room and got some iced tea and sat on the couch and smoked a cigarette. You know the rest of what happened after that point.

I would like to thank you for saving my life. I know your probably wondering how you saved my life, so I'll tell you. You saved my life by (explicit) up. There were two main (explicit) you made that saved me. The first one was the way you worded my capital murder indictment. The second was the comment you made in your closing argument when you said we won't know because he won't tell us. One more time, thank you! Now y'all know everything that happened at 8023 McLean St. on Jan. 29, 1999. I guess I forgot to mention these events when I was being questioned. Ha Ha! Sike! I knew what y'all would be able to prove in court, so I told you what you already knew.

Stacie was dead and no one else was in the house so I knew y'all would never know everything she went through unless she came back from to life. Since the supreme court said I can't be charged with capital murder again, I can tell you what I just told you because I no longer have to worry about the death penalty. And y'all are supposed to be so (explicit) smart. I can't believe y'all thought I told you everything. Well, it's too late now, nothing you can do about so (explicit) you, you fat, (explicit), (explicit), (explicit) guzzling, gutter (explicit). I guess I'll see your (explicit) on

Dec. 18 at trial because I'm not pleading to (explicit).

Tell the family to be ready to testify and relive it all again because if I have to suffer for the next 50 or 80 years or however long then they can suffer the torment of reliving what happened for a couple of days. I'm gone. (Explicit) you and anyone like you for that associates with people like you. I almost forgot, (explicit) your god, too. Jesus knows how to (explicit) a (explicit) real good. Did you teach him? Well, die a slow, painful, miserable death. See ya punk.

Do you just hate yourself for being so stupid and for (explicit) and saving me?

Sincerely,
Paul Powell

I wept for Stacie and Kristie. I was outraged and could not believe what I was reading. Powell was truly cold-hearted. He was not the least bit remorseful, and it cut me to the bone. I saw the evil, despicable (explicit) Stacie and Kristie had come face to face with. He was purely evil and dangerous. I prayed he would never be released from prison.

After a few moments sitting in silence, reflecting on this heinous letter, I realized Paul Warner Powell had signed his own death warrant. I looked up and caught Mr. Ebert's focused look. I smiled, and he grinned back. We both stood up at the same time, and I threw my arms around his neck, crying and laughing at the same time! I couldn't believe how obvious it was. I was holding Powell's hand-written letter of confession in his own words and his own handwriting in my hands.

I pulled away, looked Mr. Ebert in the eyes and said,

"We are going to nail Powell's butt to that chair after all!" I was so excited. How stupid could he possibly be? It didn't matter; he had put himself back in the chair. I told Mr. Ebert I needed to talk to Kristie and started running toward the door. I said I would call him later.

He called me back. "Lorraine, I know how excited you are about the letter, but if we are going to pursue charges of capital murder, I need you to give me back the letter. It's evidence," he said. I hadn't realized I was still holding that letter as I was running for the door. We laughed heartily over that. I raced home struggling not to speed. I couldn't wait to tell Kristie the news she needed to hear.

When I arrived home, Kristie was out with her friends. I waited for what seemed like hours, pacing the floor. When she arrived home, I told her about the letter. She asked when we could see Mr. Ebert. She wanted to read the letter herself. The next morning I called Mr. Ebert's office, and we paid him a visit. Kristie was anxious.

Powell thought because the Virginia Supreme Court overruled his conviction he was off the hook for the death penalty. I would love to have been a fly on the wall and seen his face when he learned of his own self-destruction by his "letter of confession."

## Chapter 29
# First Degree?

*"Anyone tormented by the guilt of murder will seek refuge in the grave; let no one hold them back."*
Proverbs 28:17 (ESV)

On January 13, 2003, two weeks and three days before the anniversary date of the girls' brutal attacks, we found ourselves back in court. Powell's second murder trial began. We didn't anticipate any problems. Powell had laid the ground work, and this time, it was laid in stone, again by his own hands.

Bobby was told he would be called to testify again. He adamantly stated to the court and the commonwealth attorney, he *would not* testify again. Detective Leonard paid him a visit and advised him as a witness in the case, he would be subpoenaed, and if he failed to show up for court, he would be arrested.

We had not seen Bobby in over a year, and we never spoke to each other during the trial. As he testified, I saw the same pain and suffering from the day this tragedy occurred. I realized he had never moved past that fateful day of January 29, 1999. Bobby was still wrapped up in his own grief, guilt, and suffering. Would he ever come to forgive himself?

Bobby was at the courthouse of his own free will the morning of January 13, 2003, as a witness for the second trial. As soon as he testified, he left.

With her head held high and a smile on her face, Kristie took the witness stand. She looked directly at Powell and identified him as the offender: Paul Warner Powell, who brutally attacked her. She testified a second time, while looking directly at the jury. I was very proud of Kristie. She had come a long way in four years. I was very proud of my daughter. We had united and bonded in a very special way.

The trial lasted three days. As the prosecuting attorney continued with the case, suddenly a photo of a topless young girl from a provocative magazine appeared on screen in the courtroom. I was mortified. I looked at Kristie, and she immediately looked at me. I was speechless.

I had received this photo at home, along with a hand-written message from Paul Powell from prison, taunting me. The young women in the picture vaguely resembled Stacie. She had the same color of hair and same style of haircut. I had never told Kristie about it. I immediately took the letter and picture to the prosecuting attorney's office. I told Mr. Ebert about receiving the letter from Paul Powell from prison. I was offended, angry, and furious. "Nail him to the wall!" I spewed to Mr. Ebert. "This has got to stop!"

Mr. Ebert never discussed the letter being used in his second trial. I never gave it any thought. Again my focus was on protecting my daughter. Kristie was allowed to remain in the courtroom after having testified since the second trial was only based on the charges against Powell for the murder of Stacie. The convictions against him for the abduction, rape, and attempted murder of Kristie still stood.

As soon as we were dismissed from the courtroom, the media swarmed us. I went directly to Mr. Ebert and had another angry discussion with him about the surprise attack on us. He said he thought we discussed it. I had no defense.

I pulled Kristie aside and told her about receiving the letter. She asked to what address was it sent. I told her our apartment. She was horrified. "How does he know where we live?" I assured her we were safe. The police were looking into how he found out. I was certain he had friends who were keeping him apprised of where we were. Kristie was a senior in high school, and we still lived in the area.

Paul Powell was reconvicted of capital murder of Stacie, and the jury again sentenced him to death. This time as the judge read the conviction and recommended sentencing, Powell burst into tears in an emotional melt down. I didn't buy it. Why suddenly were all the emotions? He had not beaten the justice system. He was back on death row. He would be resentenced in a few months. We won!

Kristie was doing well in school until the trial. Her grades began to suffer. She became defensive about everything and to everyone. She started staying out later and eventually wasn't coming home. I was going crazy, not knowing what was going on or where she was. She began to skip school. Our relationship began to suffer greatly. I couldn't trust her; I didn't know who she was hanging around with or where she was. We fought constantly. She wouldn't obey my rules. She ran away from home for almost a week.

I came home from work very early one day and found her sleeping. I was furious. I surprised her and demanded she get up; I was taking her to live with her dad in Arkansas. I had had enough. She was no longer going to school. He agreed to meet us in Tennessee. She didn't have much to say as we drove the nine hours to meet Tony. When we arrived, she got out of the car, took her bag, and didn't look back.

My heart hit the ground. I completely lost all control as I watched them drive away. My entire world had once again shattered into a million pieces. I was in pain, very angry, and lost. I felt I had failed Kristie and had abandoned her. I drove back to Virginia. Around 3:00 a.m., I pulled into a rest area and crawled into the back seat and slept for a couple of hours. I then drove directly to work, still wearing the same clothes from the day before.

My co-workers must have thought I had lost my mind. After days of going home to an empty apartment, the walls began to close in again. Kristie's Dad called a week later to inform me Kristie was non-compliant of his rules and was causing him to miss work. Kristie's world was completely off balance. She struggled to find this new normal that didn't yet exist.

I found out she was using drugs shortly after the second trial. She finally called and asked me if she could come home. We laid the ground rules, and she came home. The school agreed to allow her to continue her senior year. She was assigned a tutor and was home-schooled. She graduated with her class on behalf of her and her sister in May 2003. She wore both tassels on her cap!

I'm so proud of my daughter!

## Chapter 30
# Final Sentencing

*"Beloved, never avenge yourselves, but leave it to the wrath of God, for it is written, 'Vengeance is mine, I will repay, says the Lord.'"*
Romans 12:19 (ESV)

"I need to know that he's gone and that we don't have to deal with him anymore," said Kristie, now twenty-five and an advocate for rape victims. "I was totally against the death penalty before this happened, and I didn't know why people would want to do it. But they have not been through what we've been through. Now I'm totally for it. He definitely deserves to die. He needs to die for what he did to Stacie." *(Quoted in an interview with the media after Powell's second sentencing).*

The judge upheld the jury's conviction. I finally gave my impact statement to the court and Paul Powell. Looking directly at him, I expressed exactly how I felt about him, what he had done, and how much I despised him. I also told him I needed to hear him apologize and show me he had remorse for what he had done to my daughters. I waited.

He kept his eyes down on the table, completely expressionless. He had this cocky attitude and was rocking back and forth in his chair. I wanted so badly to go over there and kick the chair out from under him. His attorney, watching him intently, leaned over to him and said, "Paul, you need to show Lorraine you have remorse."

In Virginia, the defense is seated directly in front of the witness stand, about ten feet from the table. The witness stand faces the jury panel, so you're sitting at a side view from the defendant's view. Powell's eyes went from the table to the wall to his right completely avoiding me! Again, he was completely expressionless.

After the judge dismissed us from the witness stand, I walked directly to his table and got down right in his face. Behind him stood four of the largest prison guards I had ever seen, all standing at attention, ready for anything. As I approached, they moved slightly closer to Powell, ready to pounce in a heartbeat. I wasn't sure if they were worried about me or him. Kristie had accompanied me to the witness stand to read our impact statements. She had followed me, not realizing I was contemplating attacking Paul. She was ready to run to safety should he make the slightest movement. I got down in his face and said, "You have proven to me that you are the biggest coward I thought you to be!" It took all of my reserve not to reach for his throat and rip his head off in one quick motion! No one in the courtroom moved in the slightest.

As I looked and turned to go return to my seat, I caught the eye of one of the prison guards as he winked at me, as if to say, "He will get what's coming to him." I slightly smiled at him and took my seat. It was then I remembered to breathe. The courtroom was dead silent.

The Judge was looking from me to Powell as he read his sentence, and then the jury was released. He was handcuffed, put in leg shackles, and escorted from the courtroom. It was another joyous victory for us! He was going to die by execution. In the end, Powell was silent.

## Chapter 31
# Forgiveness?

*"Who has saved us and called us to a holy life —not because of anything we have done but because of his own purpose and grace. This grace was given us in Christ Jesus before the beginning of time."*
II Timothy 1:9 (ESV)

Years later my grief was still very raw. I found speaking helped to heal the wounds. I began to hear "forgiveness" being whispered. My first thought was *Why do I need to be forgiven?* Had I done something wrong? Who needed to forgive me? I was completely missing the point. I understood the Lord was speaking to *me about forgiveness*, but I was still clueless as to His point.

Once I realized the Lord was inferring that I needed to work on forgiving the perpetrator, I became furious. Although He was not intrusive or demanding but soft and subtle, I found myself getting angry at the thought of ever having to forgive Paul Powell.

I worked very hard to control my anger, yet each time I heard the Lord whisper the word, I would cringe. "Lord, how can you ask this of me? I'm fighting hard to make sure he suffers for his actions. He murdered Stacie and attempted to murder Kristie!" I gasped, "Lord, how can You ask me to forgive him of such a heinous crime against my daughters?"

God's answer was profound. "Lorraine, I sent My Son Jesus Christ to die on a cross for the very world I created. He was flogged, tormented, crucified, mocked, and nailed to a cross, while I watched them murder My only Son. Trust me!"

I will never forget those words!!

In December 2005, Kristie asked me to come to South Carolina and spend Christmas with her. Her birthday is December 26; my mother's birthday is December 25, and my maternal grandmother's was December 27. We always had a big celebration at Christmas with all three birthdays; however, everything had changed. Stacie and my grandmother were gone. Christmas would never be the same. And celebrating Kristie's birthday was very difficult.

I'd not celebrated Christmas in six years: No Christmas tree, no decorating, and no gifts. I was a volunteer Emergency Medical Technician for the Manassas Rescue Squad. I found solace in spending time answering emergency calls, and every holiday I was at the squad, where I felt I could give back to those in our community -- what so many had given to us in 1999.

I went back and forth trying to decide what to do about spending Christmas with Kristie. I had not seen her in more than two years. I had no idea where she had been or if she was okay. I desperately needed to see her but to celebrate, no! The memories were too difficult, the drive was too long, and I was needed at the squad, since the holidays always left us shorthanded. I found countless excuses as why not to go. Kristie gave up asking.

On December 24, I was on the road to South Carolina. I hadn't realized I was going until I saw the sign, "Welcome to North Carolina." I called my boss and told him I wouldn't be in the office for a couple of days. He was glad I was going.

Kristie and I spent the morning together on her birthday and then Christmas. I have to admit it was strange, especially without any other family members, Stacie or my grandmother, but it wasn't as bad as I had anticipated it would be.

I left around noon on the following day. I cried as I pulled out of her driveway, leaving her behind. She was doing well. She seemed happy. But I was in torment. My emotions ran rampant, and with a seven hour drive ahead of me that wound up being seventeen, I cried for hours. I intentionally took the longest route home up Highway 17 to avoid having to go home too soon. I had a lot of pent-up frustration. I needed the Lord to listen because I had a lot to say. I cried some more, talked, yelled, and slammed my fist against the steering wheel as angry words spewed from my lips. I laid it all out there -- all my pain and suffering. He patiently sat in the passenger seat and listened. I replayed our sixteen years with Stacie over and over in my mind. Finally, I cried out, "Lord, it's been seven years! I'm tired of fighting this battle!"

God said, "Do not be afraid or discouraged, for the battle is not yours but Mine. You do not have to fight this battle; stand firm and see the deliverance I, the Lord, will give you. I, the Lord, am with you" (paraphrased from 2 Chronicles 20:15, 17 ESV).

The Lord said I needed to surrender it all at the foot of the cross. But I told the Lord, "You need to just take it! Just take it all away!"

He responded, "You have to surrender your grief."

I argued with the Lord for several more hours on this particular issue.

He gave me scriptures about surrender. Then I heard a

holy one speaking, and another holy one said to Him, "How long will it take for the vision to be fulfilled—the vision concerning the daily sacrifice, the rebellion that causes desolation, the surrender of the sanctuary and the trampling underfoot of the LORD's people?" (Daniel 8:13, ESV)

I didn't understand at first. So I prayed and the Lord helped me to understand. We are to give our grievances to Him by laying them at the foot of the cross. I eventually laid all my burdens and heartaches at the foot of Jesus' cross, and I asked for the deliverance and peace that the Lord had said I could have.

Suddenly, I experienced the most incredible, serene feeling of freedom -- freedom from anger, depression, sorrow, and guilt. Mind you, I was driving. I felt the Lord wrap His arms around me, and I began to praise Him! Hallelujah!

The Lord said, "Look behind you."

I glanced in the rearview mirror, and I could see this enormous transparent veil blowing in the wind as I drove away. The Lord said, "This is the veil that had shrouded you in grief for seven long years." God had lifted it, and it was floating away in the wind!

Gone! What freedom! The feeling was absolutely incredible! God had answered my prayers. As I drove, I was amazed at what had just transpired. I began to reflect on the grief of the past, seeing in hindsight that grief is a true gift from the Lord. If we never experience grief, we never grow. And the Lord revealed the great power and significance in numbers. All the answers are found in God's Word through His truth. He does all things according to His will and in His timing.

I still struggled with this--forgiveness. I'd spoken to

many people about forgiveness, but I couldn't bring myself to come to that point. I had even spoken to my pastor who told me that I was not responsible for forgiving him. I really struggled with his words and went back to scripture. His response was not biblical. I lost a lot of faith in that man. However, God reminded me I was putting my trust in man. My trust needed to be in God.

I began to pray specifically for God to teach me to forgive this murderer. I knew this was something I could *NOT* do on my own. I could only do this through Him. I began seeking the Lord's divine grace and asked repeatedly for His help. One day He told me to pray for the offender. I became very angry. "Lord, I cannot, will not pray for him."

The Lord grew silent for a long period, and I realized I needed to change my attitude. I was grieving the Holy Spirit by refusing to do what the Lord had asked me to do. And so I began asking the Lord to help me to understand how to pray for him and to teach me His will. He took me to the *Book of Acts.* God showed me how to forgive, as He walked with me through the valley of the shadow of death.

Romans 12:19 says, "Do not take revenge, my dear friends, but leave room for God's wrath, for it is written: 'It is mine to avenge: I will repay,' says the Lord" (ESV). Who overcomes the world? Only those who believe that Jesus Christ is the Son of God.

One day I found myself on my knees, praying specifically for Paul. On January 29, 2008, the ninth anniversary of the girls' attack, I was lying in bed thinking about where I was nine years ago. I heard God whisper "Forgiveness, Lorraine."

Without hesitation, I responded, "Yes, Lord, I forgive Paul Powell! At that very moment, I was back in the arms of

God, standing in His throne room, surrounded by a choir of angels!

People asked me repeatedly the same question: How can God allow bad things to happen to good people. My reply is in 1 John 5:19: "We know we are children of God, and the whole world is under the control of the evil one (ESV)" Verse 20 (ESV) I John says, "We also know that the Son of God has come and has given us understanding so that we may know Him Who is true."

I forgave, but I will never forget! Just because God does allow bad things to happen to "good" people doesn't mean He has forgotten us or forsaken us. He made a promise, and God doesn't lie. He has a plan that we can't begin to fathom. If you still have doubts, read Jeremiah 29:11.

Being in the arms of the Lord is a feeling beyond comprehension. It's futile to even try to explain in words to you what it was like. I know I will always long to be in that moment, a moment of tranquility by being in Christ's arms. We will never completely know the fullness of God's blessings this side of Heaven.

## Chapter 32
# Is it Final?

*"Do not be afraid of what you are about to suffer. I tell you, the devil will put some of you in prison to test you, and you will suffer persecution for ten days. Be faithful, even to the point of death, and I will give you life as your victor's crown."*
Revelation 2:10 (ESV)

For ten years, we anticipated the execution of Paul Powell. In March 2009, we finally received the phone call we'd been waiting for. Powell's execution date finally had been set. He had exhausted all his appeals. His execution date was set for July 14, 2009. This was it.

How do you prepare for an execution? How do you prepare to watch a human being put to death by electrocution? Honestly, it wasn't a difficult decision as far as attending his execution. Kristie and I knew before the trial we would be there. Although I had forgiven Powell, the circumstances hadn't changed.

My fear was what I would see, hear, and feel in the aftermath. What kind of detrimental effects would this have on us? I prayed adamantly and asked God to protect our hearts, and minds, and to help me understand this process, and if it wasn't His will, the execution would be stopped.

I surrendered my doubts and fears to the Lord. Powell's death was due to the choices *he* made: The decisions to stalk and murder Stacie and his attempt to murder Kristie.

My family drove from Texas, and my husband and I drove from Ohio to Virginia to attend the execution. The anxiety was building, and I had a tremendous weight upon my heart, more so for Kristie should the execution be stayed for whatever reason. We arrived in Virginia and camped out at a friend's house, trying to figure out what to do with ourselves. We were next door to the nation's Capital, and sightseeing seemed a little ridicules. However, my sister is a videographer and wanted to capture footage for a documentary about our nation's Capital.

It was a beautiful day. We rode the metro rail into the city. We decided to take a self-guided tour of Washington, D.C. and found ourselves in the U.S. Capitol Building. As we were processing through security, my cell phone rang, and I immediately answered the call. It was the Virginia Department of Corrections. My heart immediately sank to my stomach.

I answered the phone and headed toward the exit, which was actually the entrance, pushing through the crowd to get outside. I ran out the door leaving behind my backpack, identification, and my family. The security officer standing at the entrance was saying something to the effect that cell phones were not permitted.

I didn't look back and heard the voice on the other end of the phone saying, "Lorraine, I am so sorry to have to tell you, but Powell's execution has been stayed."

I let out a deafening, heart-wrenching scream, "NOOOOOOO!" The security officer asked my family if I were okay. I couldn't stop repeating the words, "No! No! No! No!" My world was shattering all over again.

The caller kept apologizing. Once I got myself composed, I began to ask questions with which came no specific answers. I was advised the U.S. Supreme Court had ordered the stay of execution. Basically, we were told to go home, and if and when the execution was rescheduled, they would call.

If and when – was this all they could give us? Will there ever be justice for our family? I was told to be prepared for this possibility. How do you prepare for something you have never experienced before?

My thoughts went immediately to my daughter, Kristie. She was with friends, and I didn't want her to hear this from the news media. I called her right away and had to relay between deeps sobs of emotion that his execution had been stayed. We were given no reason.

She was furious and became very emotional. She asked me if this nightmare would ever end. I had no answers, and I couldn't hug her. It was as if we were reliving that fateful day of January 29, 1999. I began to lose hope in our justice system.

As we walked away, speechless, heads and shoulders drooped, and the day spoiled by the upsetting news, I looked up to find myself staring at the U.S. Supreme Court Building. The front of the building is engraved with the words; "EQUAL JUSTICE UNDER LAW." I was appalled. We had just been informed that the U.S. Supreme Court Justices had decided to stay the execution without a reason.

I needed to find someone to speak to about this abolition against our family, and I needed answers. It turned out the U.S. Supreme Court was closed and not even in session. How did this happen? Who made the decision? Why now? It was several years before these questions would be answered yet, never to my satisfaction.

With nothing left to do, we returned home the following

day. With my emotions spiraling out of control again, I found myself back in the early stages of grief, fighting for answers, truth, and hope. I was desperate to find anyone who was willing to talk to me.

I hadn't realized how much I had anticipated his execution. I knew then there was a lot of work I needed to do. I was a wreck emotionally and spiritually. I prayed to the Lord and tried desperately to listen. It was on the drive home when the Lord said, "Everything is in My time!" It was not God's time for Paul to be executed.

It dawned on me the Lord gave us another opportunity. Maybe I could still make this face-to-face meeting with Paul a reality. I continued writing letters and making phone calls with hopes of a face-to-face meeting with him, but he answer was "No."

In January 2010, a few weeks before the anniversary date of that fateful day, my sister, Theresa, called me and said Paul's attorney had contacted her regarding our desire to meet with Paul. She confirmed this and shared with him all the attempts made only to receive countless rejections. He said he would like to help us make that happen. She called to let me know, but I was leery.

Why did *he* want to help *us?* What was in this for him? My conception of a defense attorney wasn't a good one. Reflections of the first trial and Paul's defense attorneys put a bad taste in my mouth. Theresa felt Mr. Sheldon was sincere, but I couldn't help feeling there was more to the angle, and I was fearful Paul would find a loophole. My little sister is very thorough, and as questions arose, Theresa was contacting Mr. Sheldon to ask the whys, how comes, and what ifs.

Theresa was a huge support to me. I love her so much.

My sister's best friend, Teresa Marshall, was murdered by her husband, and Theresa followed her trial very closely, so this was a very difficult time for my sister, as well.

It became clear to us there was nothing in this for either party. Mr. Sheldon was only trying to help us with the face-to- face dialogue and get the answers we were so desperately seeking. His compassion and sympathy were not my idea of a defense attorney. I finally agreed and gave him permission to speak for our family to the governor, attorney general, and the warden, asking on our behalf to have a face-to-face meeting with Paul with Mr. Sheldon present. The answer was the same, "No!"

I struggled with the denials. What right did they have to refuse this request?

After months of trying, I finally gave in to Mr. Sheldon's offer to have a conference call in his office with Paul from the prison. At first I was completely against this idea because I was still holding out hope for a face-to-face dialogue with Paul.

Time was quickly slipping away, and in less than three months, he would be gone. On March 17, 2010, my family and I met Mr. Sheldon at his office and waited for the connection. It would take more than an hour to connect with the prison via conference call. It was excruciating waiting for the moment we would hear his voice. The anticipation was emotionally draining. The staff at the office reassured us that the problem was not on their end. It was the prison's. I never gave any thought to the hoops we had to jump through to make this call happen.

Mr. Sheldon advised the call was connected, and he was on the phone directly with Paul. He greeted Paul sincerely and asked if the attorney from the law office was with him.

Paul advised he was. Not able to hear but one side of the conversation, I was agitated at first. Finally, after the brief interview, Mr. Sheldon advised Paul that Stacie's family was present and waiting to speak with him. He inquired if Paul was ready. Paul answered he was as ready as he would ever be.

Mr. Sheldon put Paul on speaker. No one said a word, until Theresa said, "Hi Paul, this is Theresa, Lorraine's sister."

He nonchalantly replied "Hi" back. The hair on my neck stood up, and cold chills ran down my back. I wasn't expecting to feel this way. I was at peace but the sound of his voice hit several nerves.

Theresa asked how he was doing, and we received the same response as Mr. Sheldon: "I'm as good as can be expected." I wasn't quite sure how to take that comment. Were we suppose to feel sorry for him? Was this how the conversation was going to play out?

She thanked him for agreeing to the meeting. She commented we had learned he'd become a Christian and asked if he would share his journey. He agreed and said he was raised by his Christian parents, mostly his mom, but later in his young adult life, he had drifted away. He found other groups, and mostly out of curiosity, he got involved with an occult, Buddhism, and Wicca. He said that while on death row, he revisited Christianity and decided that he needed to start reading his Bible. He said it made sense. This was what he needed in his life.

His response seemed so blasé, as if no real effort was given in the decision in his relationship with Christ. I struggled with the truth of his profession. I even thought to myself, *Who is he trying to kid here*? I wasn't buying his crap.

I thought it was a joke, especially because I didn't buy into the jailhouse religion that I felt he was trying to sell us.

I began to tune him out while he rattled on. I asked the Holy Spirit to please show me if I were wrong about this. Was he really telling the truth, or was this some ploy to impress us? I heard Theresa ask him who this Pastor Paul was we had heard about, thinking it was a prison chaplain who visited him on death row and ministered to him. He laughed as if this was funny. He shared that he would send a friend scriptures and quotes. This friend would email them to his friends and family members, and the nickname became Pastor Paul.

He wasn't taking his faith seriously at all. It was one big joke to him. What a jerk! I was getting angrier by the second. But then I heard Theresa say, "Thank you Paul for sharing this with us. We want you to know we've been praying for you and your family." I waited with anticipation for his response.

He said, "Uh-huh." It wasn't gratifying. We had been praying for him. His family and I even said this in the letter I wrote explaining I had forgiven him. I really wanted to get up and leave, thinking maybe this was pointless after all.

Then something in the atmosphere changed. I was comforted and at peace. I recognized it as the presence of the Holy Spirit. For the first time during that meeting, peace washed over me. I had a feeling of strength and reassurance. The battle subsided. I looked around the room at my family to see if anyone else could feel it. No one seemed to notice. I listened, waiting for some profound statement, but all I heard was silence. I thanked the Holy Spirit for being there with us and shared my thoughts of doubts. I asked the Holy Spirit if he was being truthful with us about his faith. It wasn't what I heard but what I felt. The peace washed over me in such tranquility that I knew without a doubt Paul was telling us the truth. And I believed him from that point on. It was very clear that he, too, was a child of God.

I couldn't speak, but I wanted too. I was so drawn in by God's presence. I listened more intuitively to Paul as if I could read between the lines. When Paul conversed, it was like having a conversation with a child. He didn't express himself well or show his emotions as a man of thirty would. He had an eighth-grade education. So I began to listen through the Holy Spirit. The conversation began to make sense. I began to have compassion.

After about an hour into the call with Paul, Theresa asked Paul to walk us through that day he attacked the girls. We wanted the details in his own words. He sighed loudly, laughed nervously, and said, "Well. . . ."

He told us mostly what we already knew from the trials and the letter he wrote to Mr. Ebert in his confession. But then he brought up that he'd bought several beers, which he drank all but two while waiting at our house for Stacie to come home from school. After the argument with Stacie in the driveway, he waited a few minutes and then slipped into the house. He stashed the unopened beer bottles in Stacie's bedroom closet before going to the basement where she was doing laundry. I gasped, but only my family and Mr. Sheldon heard me. Paul continued to say that he didn't want to leave them out in the open. He meant to pick them up later on his way out the door.

Months after the girls were attacked and we'd moved back into the house, I was cleaning Stacie's room and found this brown paper bag stuffed in the back of her closet. Inside were two big bottles of beer. I was shocked to find them. As far as I knew, Stacie didn't drink. I was angry, doubtful they were hers, and yet confused. For him to mention this out of the clear blue stunned me. I had never told anyone else, not even the police. I wondered if the police had found them. If so, why weren't they dusted for finger prints, and why would they leave them in her closet? It was yet again proof he was there. But what did it matter now? He must have thought we already knew this information. However, I was glad the mystery had been solved.

Kristie hadn't said a word the entire time Paul was on the phone with us. Suddenly, she stood up, knocking the chair backward, slammed her fist into the table, and screamed into the phone at him, saying, "I have a question for you!"

Paul responded, "Okay." She spoke with venom, anger, and rage.

"I want to know why you didn't kill me, too."

Paul was silent for what seemed like a long while. Mr. Sheldon finally asked Paul if he heard Kristie's question. Still there was no answer. Mr. Sheldon looked to see if the call was still connected. It was. Then we heard what sounded like crying. It was hard to make it out, and then it became louder. Paul was sobbing. He was sobbing uncontrollably. Kristie waited, suspended over the phone. I looked at my daughter. I saw this vision: She was covered in layer upon layer of armor. She had built walls wide and thick to protect herself from her own guilt. They call it survivor's guilt. I recognized the pain in her face and her body language. She must have struggled with this question for the past eleven years. Now, she'd found the courage to ask him. How will he answer her? His sobbing subsided, and he composed himself. I looked around the table, and all of us except

Kristie were crying. I wondered if we were crying for Kristie or for both her and Paul.

Paul spoke very softly, "Kristie, I thought I had." She slowly sat back down. I looked over at her, wondering if his answer gave her any satisfaction. But what I saw gave me reassurance. I saw all that armor falling off her body, layer by layer. She took a deep breath and exhaled slowly. She seemed at peace. The battle was almost over. She was okay with his answer. He did everything in his power to kill her. But she survived. And she didn't have to wonder anymore. Tomorrow he would be dead.

My heart beat hard against my chest. I was relieved and overcome with disbelief that this had just happened. I was thankful for his answer. We all sat there in silence for a few seconds, which seemed like hours. And then I remembered I had questions. I needed answers that only he could give. However, I didn't write them down because I thought surely I could remember them. Suddenly, I couldn't remember one question I wanted to ask. Instead, I heard myself saying to him, "Paul, it's Lorraine. I wanted to speak to you face-to-face to tell you I forgave you."

"I know," he said. "I don't know what the big deal was that it didn't happen. I'm sorry. I'm sorry for putting you and your family through all this. I wish I could go back to that day. I wish I had never gone to your house. It was stupid and senseless. I think about what I did to Stacie and Kristie every day that I have been in prison. I hate myself for what I did to all of you."

I heard myself saying to Paul, "I wish you had never met my daughter. I hated you for a long time. I didn't know I could hate another human being like I hated you. But then God showed me how to forgive you. I no longer hate you. I pray for you. It wasn't an easy journey to forgiveness, Paul. It was a long difficult journey, one much like you've traveled. I suffered horrendously from guilt, just as Kristie has. I want you to know I appreciate your willingness to talk to us today. And I want you to know we will be praying you through the execution tomorrow."

"I can't believe you all have forgiven me. I don't deserve your forgiveness."

"Paul, you are a child of God, same as we are. You deserve forgiveness the same as we do. The Lord will forgive you, but you have to ask."

"No, no, no! I can't ask, and I don't deserve His forgiveness."

"Paul, as I said, it was a long journey to forgiving you. The Lord showed me that forgiveness starts with yourself. I had to work hard to forgive myself before I could ever begin to work toward forgiving you. But it was a choice and a decision to do that. A choice I made because I wanted to be set free from the bondage of sin. Unforgiveness is a sin, Paul. One we are all guilty of. And you, too, can be set free. It's your choice. I can't make it for you. No one can. But I'm praying you can find forgiveness of yourself before tomorrow night. The State of Virginia will put you to death, and you will no longer have this opportunity. God loves you, Paul. Keep that close to your heart. I know that Stacie is in heaven, and I will see her again one day. My prayer is that I will see you there."

The call ended. We couldn't call him back. The prison only allowed us two hours. We would see him at the execution in the death house.

## Chapter 33
# Amazing Grace

*"Out of his fullness we have all received grace in place of grace already given."*
John 1:16 (ESV)

We'd anticipated this day, March 18, 2010, for eleven years. And here we were. The doubts and fears began to creep in slowly. Was it really going to happen? I'd spoken to the Governor of Virginia personally a few days prior, and he assured me he would not intervene based on the information he had about the case.

I'm not going to tell you in detail about the execution again because I already have but I want you to know, it did finally happen.

The following day, Friday, March 19, 2010, we met with Governor McDonnell, thanking him for not intervening in the execution. We had requested to meet with the governor prior to the execution and were granted the day after. God had a plan, and this is the way it was to go.

We advised the governor about our countless and futile attempts to contact him personally regarding our desire to meet with Powell face-to-face before his execution. He was upset he'd not been informed of our desire to meet with him. Governor McDonnell asked how he could help us since Paul's execution had been performed. We asked that he grant victims' families and survivors the right to meet with an offender on death row, if they so desired.

Virginia Governor McDonnell agreed and amended the bill to allow face to face mediation with offender and victim(s) in Capital murder cases *£ 19.2-11.4 of the Virginia Code – Establishment of victim offender reconciliation program"* Revision of *Virginia Code* - House Bill 913... *"Establishment of a victim offender mediation program"* . . . reform measures recommended.

I was satisfied that although we would not benefit from the revision, we had paved the way for other survivors and their families who would not have to fight through the bureaucratic red tape for the right to do so. Hopefully, we'd made a small difference.

Later that day, we received a call from Mr. Sheldon, inquiring as to how we were doing? We were all still in shock having witnessed such a horrific event. Watching a human being die is excruciating, and given the matter of Paul's death, it was extremely brutal. However, I found peace and comfort in hoping Paul had found forgiveness for himself. Mr. Sheldon said he had a message for me from Paul that Paul had asked him to give me the day after his death.

He said, "Lorraine, Paul said to tell you, he forgave himself." We all burst into tears of joy and praises! He would spend eternity in heaven with our loving and gracious Father. And I know Stacie was there to welcome him home.

# Chapter 34
# Heal My Wounds,
# Leave My Scars

*"'But I will restore you to health and heal your wounds,'*
*declares the Lord."*
Jeremiah 30:17 (ESV)

Scars can be physical, emotional, or spiritual. We all have scars and a story to tell. With time, our physical wounds heal, but our emotional and spiritual wounds last a lifetime. When I reflect on my wounds, so deep and so brutal, God graciously gives me His word and truth in scriptures, such as Isaiah 53:5 *"But He was pierced for our transgressions, He was crushed for our iniquities; the punishment that brought us peace was upon Him, and by His wounds we are healed"* (ESV)

How gracious is our Lord and Savior to suffer for our sins. As God watched, His one and only Son Jesus Christ, was crucified on the cross on Calvary. As a parent, how excruciating it must have been to watch your son murdered by the very people You created. Although it was written long before Christ came to earth, God had a plan.

As I reflect on my own tragedy, I recall the notification, the denial, and the anguish that tore my heart in two. Who? Why? What did my girls do to deserve this? What kind of person could ravage this kind of anger and rage upon young girls' innocent lives?' The brutality was beyond my comprehension as a parent and as a human being. The horrific events of my daughters' attack invaded my thoughts every hour of every day and night, constantly replaying over and over again in my mind. Satan was attacking me repeatedly. I was fair game. How could I go on living? What was my purpose?

It drove me to thoughts of suicide: I wouldn't have to feel the pain any longer or relive the torture of living "hell on earth" every day.

God gently reminded me through my pain and grief that I was still a mother to Kristie, who by the grace of God, survived. She needed me now more than ever. Her survival was nothing less than a miracle, and she had not suffered any disabilities. What a testimony! God laid His hand upon her and told Satan, "She is mine!" Praise Jesus! As He revealed this to me, my life changed! I've rededicated my life to Christ. His promise stands firm in my heart always.

Each day is a new day, fashioned for each of us by God! Each new day, Kristie awakens, and this beautiful girl with big blue eyes, a laughing smile, with gorgeous features and long blonde hair, looks back at her from the mirror! What she doesn't see are the scars, so clearly visible.

Kristie doesn't hide her scars. They are there for all to see. God has given me the strength to live each day as she does. That can only come from God! Just as Thomas didn't believe Jesus had risen from the dead, he asked Jesus to prove himself. Jesus showed his scars. Thomas believed.

What began as training seminars to law enforcement officers, victims, and political science students, God created an incredible ministry: Heal My Wounds, Leave My Scars Prison Ministry. He continues to lead us to amazing places and brings extraordinary people into our lives.

I began to realize over the years that God was teaching me something – something of which I couldn't possibly begin to know. God revealed His truth throughout scriptures.

Isaiah 35:4 (ESV): "Say to those with fearful hearts, 'Be strong, do not fear; your God will come, he will come with vengeance; with divine retribution he will come to save you.'"

God led me to Acts: 16:16-40 and the story of Saul, whom God renamed Paul. Ironic? The man who committed this horrific crime against His children is also named Paul. God knew my heart, and He used this story to touch me deeply.

Though my scars were not physical but emotional, God has graciously healed my wounds and left the scars

God knows our hearts and our souls, and through Him, by our faith, love, prayers, and reading His Word, *everything is possible.* He's filled me with His Holy Spirit! Forgiveness, by the grace of God, has been granted to the person who tragically took Stacie's life and attempted to take Kristie's.

At last, I'm free from the pain and suffering. By the Father, Son, and the Holy Spirit, I'm free! Glory be to God!

Every choice has a consequence and every action has a reaction, whether positive or negative. We have the free will to choose how we will react.

My life wasn't falling apart; it was falling into place.

Chapter 35
# One Man's Soul

*"Out of his fullness we have all received grace in place of grace already given."*
John 1:16 (ESV)

As I prayed about the ending of the book, in the course of almost fifteen years, I prayed about the last chapter. I sought the Lord's desire as to how He wanted it to end. It can't end with the execution; that's too tragic. Ironic, I know. Over a course of three to four months, the Lord graciously exposed the amazing grace of our Savior.

We serve an awesome God who is to be highly exalted. We should rejoice in our sufferings and lean on Him, not our own understanding of doubts, fears, anger, rage, and hopelessness. We are the children of God, our Creator. He doesn't start something and not finish it.

There is a glorious ending to everything, and when we surrender our selfish ambition and inadequacies, His glory is revealed. Through the past fourteen years, He has shown me through trust and obedience to Him, He has a glorious plan!

The Lord walked me through the past painful memories of the girls' attack, the trials, and the execution. I began to see that one set of footprint more so than I had previously seen on those past reflections of my life's journey.

The conversation with the Lord was a revelation;

however, it was written thousands of years ago. The Lord said to me, "It wasn't always about you, Stacie, or Kristie. It was what needed to be done for the glory of My kingdom. It was about one man's soul."

One man's soul? Whose? The revelation was *Paul Powell.* I was almost knocked off my feet. The parables of the lost sheep in Matthew 18; 12-14 and Luke 15:4-7 came to mind.

Paul was one lost sheep. What was God willing to do to save one man from the pits of hell? Paul said he became a Christian and I believed him. The execution that was originally set for July 2009 was stayed and is proof to me the Lord's work wasn't complete.

The Lord's work was much bigger than I could have ever imagined. It was not about us but all about Him!

I have been called by Christ as His servant to bring forth the good news of the gospel: "To open eyes that are blind, to free captives from prison and to release from the dungeon those who sit in darkness" (Isaiah 42:7, ESV).

As a servant of Christ, we, the S.T.A.C.I.E. Foundation strives to share the gospel wherever we are called to go. In our presentation, we offer to share our testimonies through trials.

The offenders are in bondage. As a prison ministry, our job is to bring the gospel of Christ to them. In the Power Point presentation I offer, I share my testimony, the trials and tribulations and the struggles and bondage I endured, the journey with Christ through the valley of the shadow of death to the mountaintops, and the journey of forgiveness and indescribable freedom Christ has given me! I want everyone to know this freedom, and that no matter who you may be, where you are, or what you have done, when you surrender your life to Jesus Christ, *He* will change your life forever.

After we returned home from the execution, I had to attend class the following weekend. It was during that time God spoke to my heart concerning His divine calling in my life: Prison ministry. I was shocked at first, but as I begin to process His plan, it made perfect sense. Amazingly in 2009, God put on my heart to begin Heal My Wounds, Leave My Scars Prison Ministry. I assumed the Lord's desire of the ministry was to share our testimony of forgiveness.

However, God opened the doors to prison ministry when I met the founder of Heart of Texas Foundation, Grove Norwood. He invited us to Texas and the opportunity to share my testimony at two maximum security women's prisons. Since then we have received many other invitations.

## Chapter 36
# Me a Caterpillar
### By Lorraine Reed Whoberry

Before the tragedy, I was a caterpillar, truly enjoying my life of being a Mom and raising my family. I worked full time, enjoyed making and selling crafts, reading, and being outdoors. Holidays were always special; I was caught up in the excitement and magic of what was yet to come: Celebrating with family, birthdays, and embracing milestones in the girls' lives. But then on January 29, 1999, our world shattered into a million pieces. The shock and the horror of learning how to live without Stacie was extremely agonizing and wondering if Kristie would ever be Kristie again. All the things that seemed important and fun no longer mattered. We struggled to survive every second. Then came the murder trial of Paul Powell. We were again thrust into a tailspin completely out of control, slipping back into agonizing depression, torture, searing pain, and heartbreak at what was no more.

### Weaving My Cocoon

I didn't realize it then, but the moment I learned about the girls' attack, I began weaving my own cocoon. Sinking into a state of depression, Satan attempted to bury me deeper, with no plans of ever allowing me to emerge from the cocoon. But Christ's loving arms enveloped me, and He never let go. My chrysalis became Jesus' arms of protection, a place I dwelled for nine years. It was during this time, I was transformed into a new me. As it says in Ecclesiastes 3:1-8, *There is a time for everything, a season for every activity under the heavens; a time to be born and a time to die, a time to plant and a time to uproot, a time to kill and a time to heal, a time to tear down and a time to build, a time to weep and a time to laugh, a time to mourn and a time to dance, a time to scatter stones and a time to gather them a time to embrace and a time to refrain, a time to search and a time to give up, a time to keep and a time to throw away, a time to tear and a time to mend, a time to be silent and a time to speak, a time to love and a time to hate, a time for war and a time for peace* (NIV). God transformed the old me into a new person. The old me died the day of the girls' attack, God healed my wounds but left my scars.

## Emerging

The time came to emerge from my cocoon. I was ready to spread my wings, but the journey proved to be a slow process, and while the transformation was gradual, it was miraculous as to what God had been up to in my life. I was sinking into the pits of hell, but Christ wrapped me in His loving embrace and transformed me into a warrior. I sang His praises, stood on His promises, and now live for the Kingdom of Heaven. This stage of my journey was complete. I learned a valuable lesson during my incubation period: Grief is a treasurable gift from God.

During this chapter of my journey I learned to embrace Christ like never before. He fought for us in the biggest battle of our lives. And then to discover, it wasn't just us He fought for, He fought for Paul Powell's soul. Paul received his wings on March 18, 2010.

# Final Thoughts

Not a day goes by that I don't think about Stacie and the horror and fear my girls faced on January 29, 1999. Stacie, in an attempted rape, was ripped from our lives, murdered at the age of sixteen. Kristie's attack was extremely brutal, yet her perseverance to survive was stronger than the grip of death. I've always told her that God had His hands on her that fateful day, and He has a special purpose for her life. She's a miracle.

The horror my precious daughters suffered at the hands of a murderer, plagued by hatred and prejudice, is beyond our comprehension. How can someone hate so viciously?

We will never understand what drove Paul Powell to do what he did. And I don't agree when people tell me, "It was Stacie's time to go." No it wasn't! By all rights, she should still be here. What right did he have to do what he did to Stacie, Kristie, our family, and our communities in a brutal outrage on a path to destruction? None!

Suffering was not on my agenda nor my family's. I realized I had to figure out a way to survive. The Lord was there to help us through the darkest times. He brought people into our lives who could pick us up, hold us up, allow us to fall into their arms and lean against them as we struggled to find our balance once again. We have met some incredible people through this tragedy. These angels in disguise came at just the right moments. Some are here for a lifetime, others for brief, fleeting moments. When we needed God most, He was there in the hearts and souls of those He sent as His angels! They were there to take Stacie home, and they were there to bring us comfort. They lifted our wounded hearts to God, and He answered them profoundly! I've come to realize this wasn't just our tragedy; it was everyone's tragedy.

*You felt our pain;*
*God heard your cries.*

*You prayed for us when*
*we couldn't find our voices.*

*God answered and*
*gave us peace and comfort.*

*Although we didn't see you,*
*we knew you were there.*

*Some of you we were blessed to meet,*
*others stood in the background and shadows.*

*We want to thank everyone for*
*surrounding us with love, compassion, and prayers.*

*Without your support, we wouldn't be where we are or*
*the people we've become today.*

*Because you cared and prayed,*
*we've survived!*

*God bless you, and we praise God for each of you!*

# Who Stacie was to her friends...

Stacie was a friend, neighbor, and she was my friend. She swam with me, always remembered and celebrated my birthday. Our families had lots of cookouts together. One summer I had a fourth of July party, and we went to Costella Park to see the fireworks. We also ordered crabs.

"Stacie, I feel shocked and feel very sad and upset with the guy. Thank you for talking to me and helping me walk in my gait trainer. She reminded me to walk daily. The pin I wear is really helping me because it makes me think she's with me like my guardian angel. Stacie, I miss you very much. I love you.

Travis

Travis and Stacie attended high school together. Travis is wheelchair bound and mentally challenged. His dad threw his mom down a flight of stairs in an attempt to abort Travis. He suffered severe brain damage. Stacie didn't see Travis' disabilities. She saw him as one of her many best friends.

🐸🐸🐸

The day I moved into the Bull Run Trailer Park, I didn't know anybody. I used to ride my bike until one day I met this girl, Stacie. Ever since that day we would do things together. If I wasn't at her house, she was at mine. We shared a lot together until the day she moved. I didn't see her much since it was a long walk to her house.

The day she found out I was pregnant, she was by my

side. She said she was going to be an aunt since we were such good friends. Stacie was like a sister to me. When my son was five days old, tragedy struck. I was sitting in my hospital room with my little son when I heard the news. I cried and cried. I just couldn't help myself. I didn't want to believe it. But now she is in heaven looking down on my son, Byron, and telling herself that she's now an aunt. The good thing is that she knew he was born.

Love

Loressa

Goodbye Friend

Stacie, why this happened, I don't know but it hurts so much to let you go! You were there for me when I needed you! We had our faults, yes, but always worked them out. You treated me like a sister, and I looked up to you. We told each other our secrets and vowed never to tell. I felt I could tell you anything. I know you're really gone in body but in spirit, no!

I will always hold the memories of you in my heart, and I am sorry that this happened to such a dear sweet person as yourself, but always remember that I miss you, and I'm still your friend.

Love always, your best friend,

Allyson

Stacie you treated me like a little brother. You were always there for me when I needed you, and I thank you for everything, and I'll see you when I get there!

Love Always, your Lil Brother,

Kevin

Hey girl, we all miss you so much! You were always there for me when I needed to talk to someone. You were one of the nicest people, I think, in the whole school. You were always making friends and helping people out when they needed you. We had some fun times in middle school. Remember the big food fight in the eighth grade? Well I just wanted to write you and say a formal goodbye. I will always remember you! ☺

P.S. I miss you…

Love always.

Camille

Stacie was nice, and she was my friend, and I miss her.

Adam

Stacie, Hey Girly! It's me. We were never really the best of friends, and I know we had our times, but you know I will always be thinking of you and how you always made me laugh in class and how good you always smelled!

Master Sergeant won't leave me alone about the fight we had. He said you were about to "fire me up!" I miss you a lot, and I feel so bad about the fight. I wish I could have said I was sorry before you were gone. I hope you'll forgive me like I forgive you. You know I'll always think of you, and we'll always miss you.

Goodbye for now…Always,

Melissa

I think you already know how I feel. But believe me when I say it will get easier as life goes on. I hope that Paul gets what is coming to him!

Your friend,

Eric

Dear Ms. Reed,

I wish to express our deepest condolences on the tragic loss of your daughter, Stacie Lynn. She worked for us for only a few short weeks, but she made a deep impression on everyone who came in contact with her. She will be remembered as a happy, bright, and capable young woman with a promising future.

On behalf of all us at Popeye's, we wish you Godspeed and comfort in making sense of this tragedy.

Sincerely,

David J. Rosenstein

President

Stacie's Mom,

I received a type-written essay that Stacie wrote in one of her eighth grade classes, given to me by one of Stacie's teachers after she was killed. . . .

The person who has made the biggest impact on my life, I would have to say, it would be my mom. She has always been there for me even when I didn't want her there.

She taught me to be a kind person and show myself, as well as others, respect. As she would say, "Treat others as you would want to be treated."

If it wasn't for having her in my life, I don't know where I would be right now. I never learned until this year how much she actually cared about me and how much pain and suffering I put her through over the years. What amazes me the most about my mom is that she was always by my side and in my heart! I don't know if it's just a motherly instinct or what, but she would always know if I were in trouble or hurt. She would always find some way to get to me.

I don't think I will ever understand how much she cares and understands me until I actually grow up and have kids. I am glad to have a Mom that cares about where I'm at, who I'm with, and what time I'll be home, instead of having a Mom who doesn't care.

She always taught me not to be racist to anyone and that we were all created the same. She also taught me that if I wanted something, to go out there and get it, to never give up hope.

We've had our ups and downs, but what mother, daughter hasn't? I'm really glad that we finally learned to talk and work our differences out, instead of getting mad and yelling at each other. I hope twenty years from now, she can show her grandchildren this letter, and maybe one day they will understand how much I care about them, the way my mother cared about me.

Stacie

These letters have touched my heart repeatedly. I miss my daughter so much! She will not be forgotten as just another victim of homicide; she will always be remembered for the legacy she left all of us. Oh, to be the person God designed us to be.

# PTSD

From *The Ohio Domestic Violence Network*

**What is Post Traumatic Stress Disorder or PTSD?** It is a normal emotional and psychological reaction to trauma (a painful, shocking, experience, such as rape, war, natural disaster) that is outside of a person's normal life experiences.

**Why should I learn about PTSD?** Because you or someone you know may experience trauma at some time in your life! Learning about PTSD can help you cope with trauma and/or help others.

**Who is likely to suffer from PTSD?** Anyone who experiences a traumatic event. PTSD can affect survivors of war, violent attacks, rape, car or plane accidents, and natural disasters or can affect people who witness these events.

**Symptoms may include**
Anxiety - Avoiding anything that reminds the survivor of the incident.
Insomnia - Recurrent memories or flashbacks of the trauma.
Irritability - Difficulty concentrating or focusing.
Feeling numb - Hyper-vigilance (feeling "on guard" all the time).
Survivor guilt - Lack of interest in family, friends, or hobbies
Nightmares - Jumpiness (especially at loud or sudden

noises).

Restlessness - They may also suffer from depression, blame themselves, or become suicidal.

Overwhelming emotions - Feeling as though they are "going crazy."

Fear "something bad" will happen - Difficulty sleeping

# Recovery from PTSD Takes Time

Survivors recover in stages. They may start with one stage, go to another, and go back. Each person processes the event his or her own way.

Here are some stages a survivor may go through.

1. Denial that the rape/attack had any effect on his/her life.
2. Fear it will happen again.
3. Feel sad because of a loss of his/her ability to trust people or places.
4. Anger at what happened.
5. Anxiety over the nightmares or flashbacks that may intrude on the life of the survivor.
6. Feel as if a part of themselves died during the rape/attack.

Survivors are not to blame for the crime committed to them by another person. We cannot control the actions of another person.

Survivors need a safe environment to work through their fears. You can help provide that environment by reading all you can on PTSD and allowing the survivor space and time to recover. If you are someone close to a survivor, you also may want to check into counseling, or find someone you can talk to.

# There is a Future After Trauma

Kristie and Jason's Wedding Day.

You may wondering how Kristie is doing today. I'm thrilled to tell you she's doing wonderfully. She's a pillar of strength and my hero. She's an awesome wife and an amazing mother to our two beautiful grandchildren. Her healing was a slow and agonizing process, through which she has persevered. She's overcome enormous obstacles and hurdles that far exceed the tragedy she suffered so many years ago. I'm so very proud of my daughter.

Lorraine

# Step Out in Faith

For more than eleven years, our family endured countless motions, hearings, two capital murder trials, and appeals. For seven years, I struggled with grief, shock, denial, guilt, anguish, thoughts of suicide, anxiety, and depression. However, it was during these struggles I recognized God's presence.

In 2006, I moved from Virginia to Ohio and shortly thereafter enrolled in the ABC/Ohio Pastoral Leadership Program in answer to the Lord's calling. That would inevitably change my life forever. It was while in my third year of the program, the Lord revealed His plan: Prison Ministry. Honestly, this was the last place I wanted to go.

I began praying, asking the Lord to reveal why His desire was prison ministry. He showed me His glory. Amazingly, during those deep dark periods of pain and suffering, Christ was preparing me.

On March 17, 2010, via a conference call from his attorney's office to the prison, we spoke to Paul Powell for the first time in eleven years. Although we were very apprehensive about the meeting, we talked for three hours.

My sister was our mediator and asked him to share his testimony, which he did, yet I was very skeptical--but listened intently.

I realized it wasn't what I was hearing; it was what I was feeling--Christ's presence and His peace. Christ was there with us! And suddenly, I knew Paul was sincere in what he, too, had experienced. I related to the story of Acts in the Bible, which I had done some many times before with my own struggles since that fateful day in January 1999. I finally spoke up and asked Paul a question regarding his forgiveness of himself. He shouted "No!" I continued to speak to him and got no response. He was going to meet Jesus Christ the following night. Was he ready to face his Creator? He was quiet, then we heard him softly crying, and then we cried for him and with him. I told him we were praying for him and would continue to pray for him and asked him to pray also for God's peace.

The moment the call ended I realized God had been testing me. I needed to step out in faith and trust Him completely. I had done exactly what God desired of me. I left the office again with a very profound sense of peace. I knew where Paul was going, and I knew we would be okay.

Through the ministry I have been called by Christ as His servant to bring forth the good news of the gospel. "To open eyes that are blind, to free captives from prison and to release from the dungeon those who sit in darkness" (Isaiah 42:7, ESV). As a servant of Christ, we share the gospel in a Power Point presentation called **HOPE!** *The cross is the anchor of Hope in the midst of trouble.* Jesus Christ is our only hope. By His birth, death, and resurrection, we are redeemed through His sacrifice on the cross.

These offenders are in bondage. As a prison ministry, our job is to bring the gospel of Christ to them. In the Power Point presentation I offer, I share my testimony: The trials and tribulations, the struggles and bondage I endured, the journey with Christ through the valley of the shadow of death to the mountaintops. I describe the journey of forgiveness and indescribable freedom Christ has given me!

I want everyone to know this freedom and that no matter who you are, where you are, or what you have done, when you surrender your life to Jesus Christ, He will change your life forever.

I share this with you because after I returned home from the execution, I had to attend class the following weekend. It was during that time God spoke to my heart about His divine calling in my life --Prison Ministry. I was shocked at first, but as I began to process His plan, it made perfect sense. What's so amazing is that in 2009, God put on my heart to begin "Heal My Wounds, Leave My Scars Ministry." I thought the ministry was to share my testimony to churches. However, God opened the doors to prison ministry and gave me the opportunity to share my testimony in two maximum security prisons in Texas, and the Franklin Pre-Release Center in Columbus. Since then we have received other invitations as well.

I believe a ministry has to have a solid foundation based on scriptures: Luke 14:29, 33. A solid foundation has to have a cornerstone. The cornerstone is Jesus Christ. Heal My Wounds, Leave My Scars Ministry, is Christ's ministry and without Christ and the Church, there is no ministry.

*"The LORD make his face shine on you and be gracious to you; the LORD turn his face toward you and give you peace."*
Numbers 6:25-26 (ESV)

www.Staciefoundation.org

Please feel free to write to us at
PO Box 317747
Cincinnati, OH 45231

CPSIA information can be obtained
at www.ICGtesting.com
Printed in the USA
FFHW021503130519
52425243-57851FF